D1718316

**EDITIONS FAVRE SA**

**Headquarters**
29, rue de Bourg
CH-1003 Lausanne
Tel +41 (0)21 312 17 17
Fax +41 (0)21 320 50 59
lausanne@editionsfavre.com

**Paris office**
7, rue des Canettes
F-75006 Paris
www.editionsfavre.com

Legal registration in
Switzerland in 2014.
All rights reserved for all
countries. All reproduction,
even partial, by any means
whatsoever, is prohibited.

ISBN 978-2-8289-1472-1

© 2014, by Editions Favre SA,
Lausanne, Switzerland

© Original copyright:
Bertrand Piccard
et André Borschberg

FAVRE

# SOLAR**IMPULSE**

—

**ROUND-THE-WORLD COUNTDOWN**

**OBJECTIF TOUR DU MONDE**

STARTKLAR ZUR WELTUMRUNDUNG

# CONTENTS
# SOMMAIRE
# INHALTSVERZEICHNIS

A UNIQUE AIRPLANE WITH UNLIMITED ENDURANCE FLYING **DAY AND NIGHT WITH NO FUEL.**

UN AVION UNIQUE À L'AUTONOMIE ILLIMITÉE QUI VOLE **JOUR ET NUIT SANS CARBURANT.**

EIN EINZIGARTIGES FLUGZEUG MIT UNBEGRENZTER AUTONOMIE, DAS **TAG UND NACHT OHNE TREIBSTOFF** FLIEGEN KANN.

—

A TEAM **DRIVEN BY A VISION
OF THE FUTURE** AND A
**PASSION FOR INNOVATION.**

UNE ÉQUIPE **PORTÉE PAR
UNE VISION** D'AVENIR ET
UNE **PASSION DE L'INNOVATION.**

EIN TEAM MIT EINER **VISION FÜR
DIE ZUKUNFT** UND EINER
**LEIDENSCHAFT FÜR INNOVATION.**

ATTEMPTING THE **FIRST SOLAR FLIGHT AROUND THE WORLD.**

POUR TENTER LE **PREMIER VOL SOLAIRE AUTOUR DU MONDE.**

EIN VERSUCH, **DIE WELT** ERSTMALIG IN EINEM SOLARFLUGZEUG **ZU UMRUNDEN.**

**EXPLORING** NEW WAYS OF DOING AND THINKING, TO **ACHIEVE THE IMPOSSIBLE.**

**EXPLORER** DE NOUVELLES FAÇONS DE FAIRE ET DE PENSER POUR **RÉALISER L'IMPOSSIBLE.**

NEUE METHODEN UND DENKWEISEN **ENTDECKEN,** DIE DAS **UNMÖGLICHE MÖGLICH MACHEN.**

SENDING A MESSAGE TO **INSPIRE
PRESENT AND FUTURE GENERATIONS.**

TRANSMETTRE UN MESSAGE
POUR **INSPIRER LES GÉNÉRATIONS
ACTUELLES ET FUTURES.**

EINE BOTSCHAFT VERMITTELN,
DIE **HEUTIGE UND ZUKÜNFTIGE
GENERATIONEN INSPIRIERT.**

PROVIDING **SOLUTIONS TO THE CHALLENGES** OUR PLANET NOW FACES.

PROPOSER DES **SOLUTIONS AUX DÉFIS** ACTUELS DE **NOTRE PLANÈTE.**

**LÖSUNGSANSÄTZE** FÜR DIE AKTUELLEN **HERAUSFORDERUNGEN** UNSERES PLANETEN BIETEN.

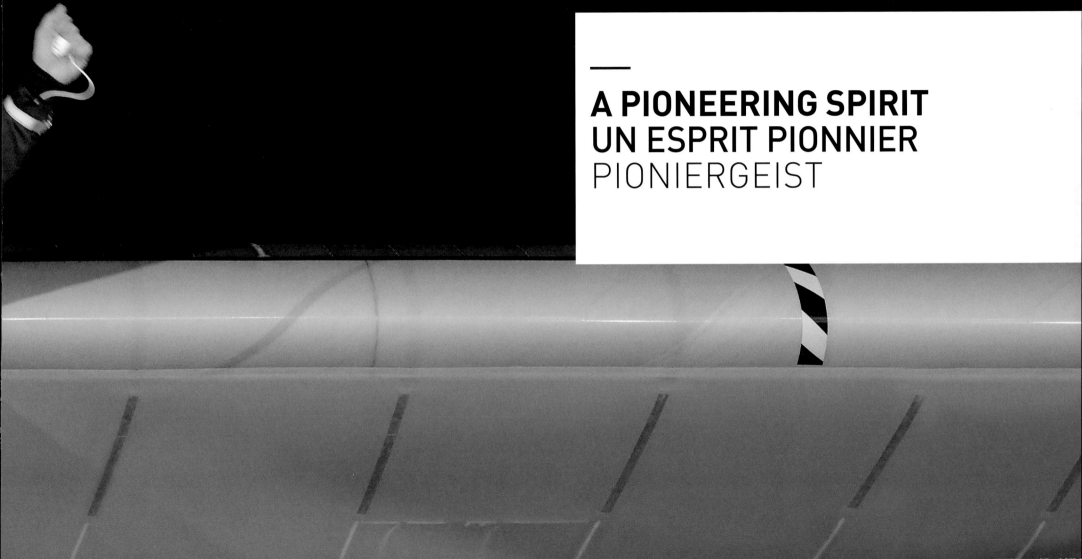

# A PIONEERING SPIRIT
## UN ESPRIT PIONNIER
PIONIERGEIST

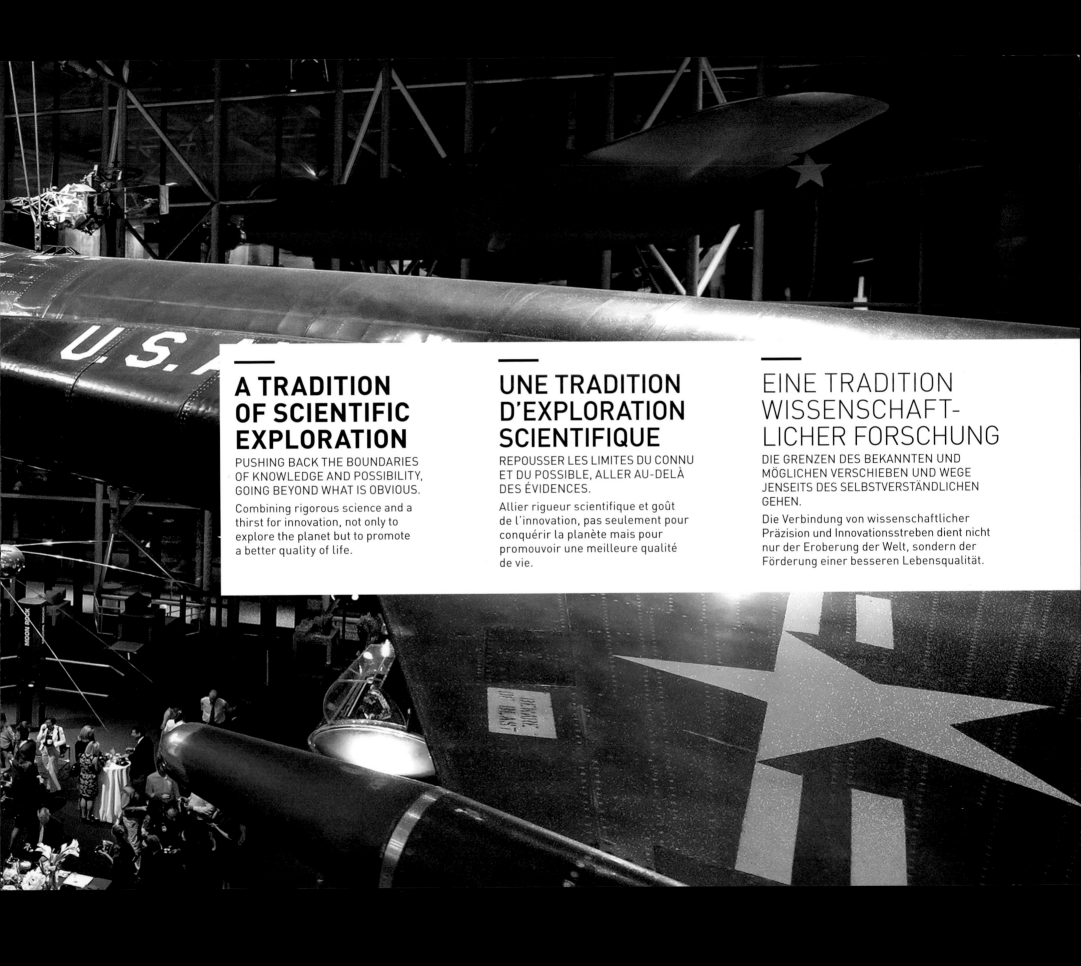

## A TRADITION OF SCIENTIFIC EXPLORATION

PUSHING BACK THE BOUNDARIES OF KNOWLEDGE AND POSSIBILITY, GOING BEYOND WHAT IS OBVIOUS.

Combining rigorous science and a thirst for innovation, not only to explore the planet but to promote a better quality of life.

## UNE TRADITION D'EXPLORATION SCIENTIFIQUE

REPOUSSER LES LIMITES DU CONNU ET DU POSSIBLE, ALLER AU-DELÀ DES ÉVIDENCES.

Allier rigueur scientifique et goût de l'innovation, pas seulement pour conquérir la planète mais pour promouvoir une meilleure qualité de vie.

## EINE TRADITION WISSENSCHAFT-LICHER FORSCHUNG

DIE GRENZEN DES BEKANNTEN UND MÖGLICHEN VERSCHIEBEN UND WEGE JENSEITS DES SELBSTVERSTÄNDLICHEN GEHEN.

Die Verbindung von wissenschaftlicher Präzision und Innovationsstreben dient nicht nur der Eroberung der Welt, sondern der Förderung einer besseren Lebensqualität.

# THREE GENERATIONS | TROIS GÉNÉRATIONS | DREI GENERATIONEN

### AUGUSTE PICCARD

**Explorer of the stratosphere, the first man to see the curvature of the earth, he paved the way for modern aviation.**

Explorateur de la stratosphère, premier homme à voir la courbure de la terre, il ouvre la voie à l'aviation moderne.

Erforscher der Stratosphäre und der erste Mensch, der die Krümmung der Erde gesehen hat. Er ebnet den Weg für die moderne Luftfahrt.

### JACQUES PICCARD

**Deepest man on earth, pioneer of scientific ecology, dedicated to protecting seas and lakes.**

Homme le plus profond du monde, pionnier de l'écologie scientifique, dévoué à la protection des mers et des lacs.

Pionier der Ökologie-Wissenschaften und der Mensch, der den tiefsten, je unternommenen Tauchgang vollbracht hat. Er widmet sich dem Schutz der Meere und Seen.

### BERTRAND PICCARD

**Explorer with a philosophical vision seeking to promote the pioneering spirit and innovation in everyday life.**

Un explorateur à la vision humaniste qui s'attache à promouvoir l'esprit pionnier et l'innovation dans la vie de tous les jours.

Ein Forscher mit humanistischem Weltbild. Er verschreibt sich der Förderung von Pioniergeist und Innovation im Alltag.

The invention of the pressurized cabin and the first ascent into the stratosphere in 1931, reaching an altitude of 52,000 feet.

L'invention de la cabine pressurisée et la première ascension dans la stratosphère en 1931, atteignant une altitude de 16 000 mètres.

Erfindung der Druckkabine und erster Aufstieg in die Stratosphäre im Jahr 1931 auf eine Höhe von 16 000 Meter.

The invention of the bathyscaphe and the record dive to the bottom of the Mariana Trench at 36,000 feet.

L'invention du bathyscaphe et la plongée record au fond de la Fosse des Mariannes à 10 916 mètres.

Erfindung des Bathyscaph und Rekordtauchgang in die Tiefen des Marianengrabens auf 10 916 Meter.

First non-stop balloon flight around the world, and the longest flight in distance and duration in the history of aviation, 27,900 miles in 20 days.

Premier tour du monde en ballon sans escale, vol le plus long en distance et en durée de toute l'histoire de l'aviation. 45 000 kilomètres en 20 jours.

Erste Nonstop-Weltumrundung in einem Heißluftballon. Längster Flug im Hinblick auf Flugstrecke und Flugdauer sowie in der Geschichte der Luftfahrt. 45 000 Kilometer in 20 Tagen.

**1905**

**Invention of the bathyscaphe principle**

Invention du principe du bathyscaphe

Erfindung des Bathyscaph-Prinzips

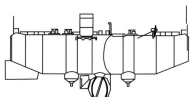

**1931**

**Stratospheric balloon FNRS**

Ballon stratosphérique FNRS

Stratosphären-Ballon FNRS

**1948**

**Bathyscaphe FNRS2**

Bathyscaphe FNRS2

Bathyscaph FNRS2

**1960**

**Bathyscaphe Trieste**

Bathyscaphe Trieste

Bathyscaph Trieste

**1964**

**Mesoscaphe Auguste Piccard, first submarine for tourists**

Mésoscaphe Auguste Piccard, premier sous-marin touristique

Mesoscaph Auguste Piccard, das erste, für touristische Zwecke gebaute U-Boot

**1999**

**Orbiter 3 balloon**

Ballon Orbiter 3

Heißluftballon Orbiter 3

**1900**          **1920**          **1940**          **1960**          **1980**          **2000**

# WRITING HISTORY | ÉCRIRE L'HISTOIRE | GESCHICHTE SCHREIBEN

**Curiosity, a need to understand the world, respect for nature and faith in technological solutions.**

La curiosité, le besoin de comprendre le monde, le respect de la nature et la foi dans les solutions technologiques.

Neugier, das Bedürfnis, die Welt zu verstehen, Respekt vor der Natur und der Glaube an technologische Lösungen.

**CARRYING ON A TRADITION OF EXPLORATION IN A SHARED ADVENTURE, COMBINING PROGRESS AND SUSTAINABILITY.**

**PERPÉTUER UNE TRADITION D'EXPLORATION DANS UNE AVENTURE À PARTAGER MÊLANT PROGRÈS ET DURABILITÉ.**

DIE FORSCHERTRADITION MIT EINEM GEMEINSAMEN ABENTEUER FORTSCHREIBEN, DAS FORTSCHRITT UND NACHHALTIGKEIT MITEINANDER VERBINDET.

## DUAL CONTROL

TWO MEN, PIONEERS AND INNOVATORS, PAIR UP FOR A GROUNDBREAKING ADVENTURE.

Their very different approaches complement each other for greater creativity. Bertrand Piccard brings his avant-gardist mindset and André Borschberg his entrepreneurial experience.

## UN TANDEM AUX COMMANDES

DEUX HOMMES, PIONNIERS ET INNOVATEURS, ASSOCIÉS POUR RÉALISER UNE AVENTURE HORS DES SENTIERS BATTUS.

Des approches très différentes qui se complètent pour atteindre plus de créativité. Bertrand Piccard apporte sa vision avant-gardiste et André Borschberg, son expérience d'entrepreneur.

## EIN TANDEM AM STEUER

ZWEI MÄNNER, PIONIERE UND INNOVATOREN, SCHLIESSEN SICH FÜR EIN ABENTEUER JENSEITS DER AUSGETRETENEN PFADE ZUSAMMEN.

Zwei ausgesprochen verschiedene Ansätze, die sich ergänzen, um noch kreativer zu sein. Bertrand Piccard steuert seine avantgardistischen Visionen bei und André Borschberg seine Erfahrung als Unternehmer.

### BERTRAND PICCARD
**Keen to promote clean technologies, he develops the project's symbolic and political reach and brings in the partners financing this challenge.**

Désireux de promouvoir les technologies propres, il développe la portée symbolique et politique du projet et réunit les partenaires qui financent ce défi.

In seinem Bestreben, saubere Technologien zu fördern, entwickelt er die symbolische und politische Dimension des Projektes und bringt die finanziellen Partner dieser Herausforderung zusammen.

### ANDRÉ BORSCHBERG
**His sound managerial experience and interest in innovative solutions have led him to spearhead the technical and operational team.**

Sa solide expérience de manager et son intérêt pour les solutions nouvelles l'ont amené à diriger l'équipe technique et opérationnelle.

Mit seiner umfassenden Erfahrung als Manager und seinem Interesse an innovativen Lösungen leitet er das technische und operative Team.

**THE SYNERGY BETWEEN THE PSYCHIATRIST-EXPLORER AND THE ENGINEER-ENTREPRENEUR.**

LA SYNERGIE ENTRE LE PSYCHIATRE EXPLORATEUR ET L'INGÉNIEUR ENTREPRENEUR.

EINE SYNERGIE ZWISCHEN FORSCHENDEM PSYCHIATER UND UNTERNEHMERISCHEM INGENIEUR.

**Fighter pilot and balloon pilot will take turns at the controls of Solar Impulse.**

Le pilote de chasse et le pilote de ballon se relaient aux commandes de Solar Impulse.

Jagdpilot und Ballonfahrer wechseln sich am Steuer von Solar Impulse ab.

### A MULTI-DISCIPLINARY TEAM

PROFESSIONALS FROM ALL
BACKGROUNDS SEEKING ORIGINAL
SOLUTIONS FOR ACHIEVING
THE IMPOSSIBLE.

More than 90 people in all professions,
from engineering to operations and
from construction to communication.

### UNE ÉQUIPE MULTI-DISCIPLINAIRE

DES PROFESSIONNELS DE TOUS
HORIZONS S'EFFORÇANT DE TROUVER
DES SOLUTIONS INÉDITES POUR
RÉALISER L'IMPOSSIBLE.

Plus de 90 personnes rassemblant
tous les métiers, de l'ingénierie aux
opérations, en passant par la
construction et la communication.

### EIN MULTI-DISZIPLINÄRES TEAM

EXPERTEN ALLER ART BEMÜHEN SICH,
BEISPIELLOSE LÖSUNGSANSÄTZE
ZUR ERREICHUNG DES UNMÖGLICHEN
ZU FINDEN.

Mehr als 90 Personen aus allen
beruflichen Bereichen: Ingenieur-
wissenschaften, operatives Geschäft,
Konstruktionstechnik und Kommunikation.

**THEY'VE DONE IT!
YESTERDAY, IT WAS A DREAM;
TODAY, IT'S A REVOLUTIONARY
AIRPLANE.**

ILS L'ONT FAIT!
HIER, C'ÉTAIT UN RÊVE;
AUJOURD'HUI, C'EST UN
AVION RÉVOLUTIONNAIRE.

SIE HABEN ES GESCHAFFT!
GESTERN WAR ES NOCH
EIN TRAUM, HEUTE IST ES EIN
REVOLUTIONÄRES FLUGZEUG.

**ALL DETERMINED TO ACHIEVE WHAT WAS THOUGHT IMPOSSIBLE. IF IT WAS EASY, EVERYONE WOULD HAVE ALREADY DONE IT!**

TOUS ENGAGÉS À RÉALISER CE QUE L'ON CROYAIT IMPOSSIBLE. SI C'ÉTAIT FACILE, TOUT LE MONDE L'AURAIT DÉJÀ ACCOMPLI!

ALLE SETZEN SICH DAFÜR EIN, DAS UNMÖGLICHE MÖGLICH ZU MACHEN. WENN ES EINFACH WÄRE, HÄTTE ES BEREITS JEMAND GEMACHT!

### A FAMILY

A SHARED VISION FOR
CLEAN TECHNOLOGY AND
RENEWABLE ENERGY.

Committed partners, famous
patrons and enthusiastic
supporters, all promoting
this futuristic adventure.

### UNE FAMILLE

UNE VISION PARTAGÉE AUTOUR
DES TECHNOLOGIES PROPRES ET
DES ÉNERGIES RENOUVELABLES.

Des partenaires engagés,
des parrains prestigieux et
des supporters enthousiastes,
tous promoteurs de cette
aventure futuriste.

### EINE FAMILIE

EINE GEMEINSAME VISION FÜR
SAUBERE TECHNOLOGIEN UND
ERNEUERBARE ENERGIEN.

Engagierte Partner, angesehene
Paten und begeisterte Supporter.
Sie alle sind Förderer dieses
zukunftsträchtigen Abenteuers.

# **PARTNERS** | **PARTENAIRES** | PARTNER

**Solvay**
13 plastic products in 25 applications plus 6,000 parts to lighten the whole structure of the airplane.

**Omega**
A test bench to improve the efficiency of the motors at all temperatures.

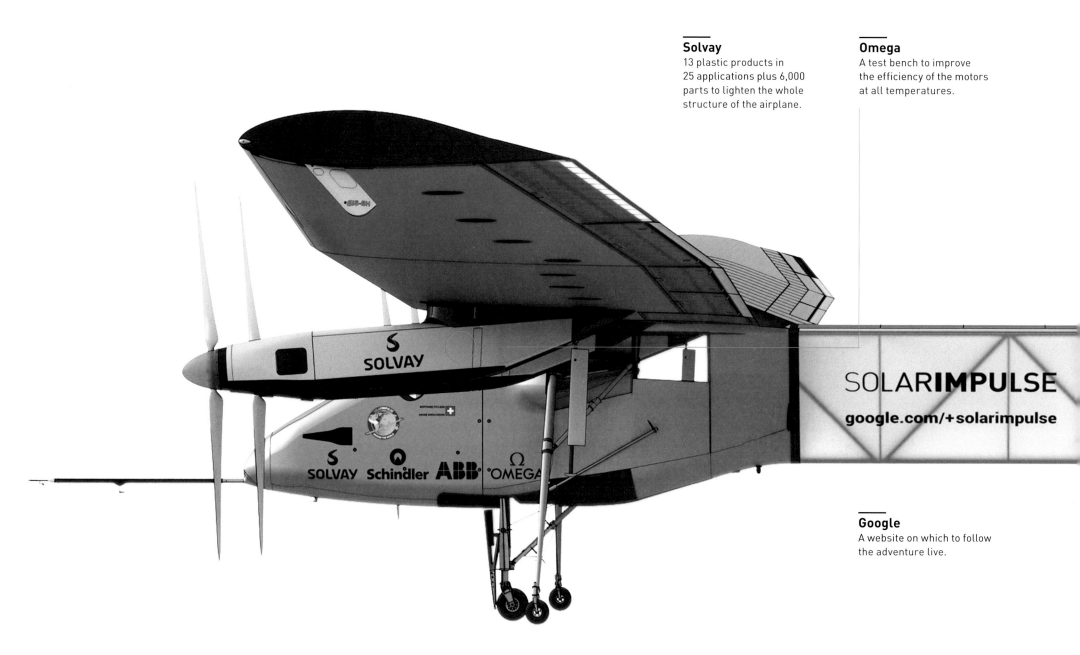

**Google**
A website on which to follow the adventure live.

### Schindler

Engineers embedded in the Solar Impulse team to stimulate research and development in new technologies in areas from applied electronics to advanced structures.

### ABB

Energy-saving current regulators and technologies to improve energy efficiency in systems along the whole propulsion chain – from source to distribution.

### Bayer MaterialScience

Nanotechnologies to increase the strength of the materials.

### Swiss Re Corporate Solutions

Full insurance coverage for a high-risk project and actions to alert the media and the public to the consequences of climate change.

### Altran

Several engineers for project launch and ongoing management, as well as the development of the route modelling and flight-trajectory simulations needed for mission flight-planning.

### Swiss Confederation

Diplomatic relations facilitating contacts with authorities and opening access to airspace over foreign territories.

### Masdar

Hosting the team and the airplane in Abu Dhabi, for the departure and the arrival of the round-the-world flight, a way to demonstrate common values for renewable energy.

### Decision
Construction of all large carbon-fiber parts by processes giving a lighter structure than any seen before.

### Solvay
Encapsulation of solar cells in a waterproof UV resistant resin.

### SunPower
Solar cells as thin as a human hair.

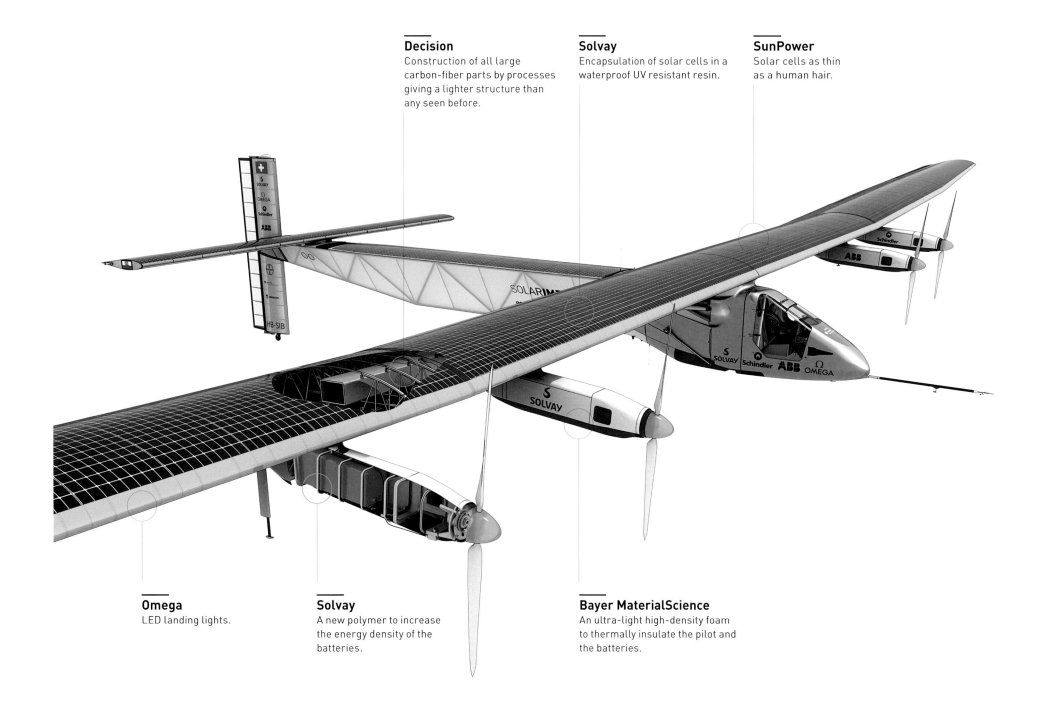

### Omega
LED landing lights.

### Solvay
A new polymer to increase the energy density of the batteries.

### Bayer MaterialScience
An ultra-light high-density foam to thermally insulate the pilot and the batteries.

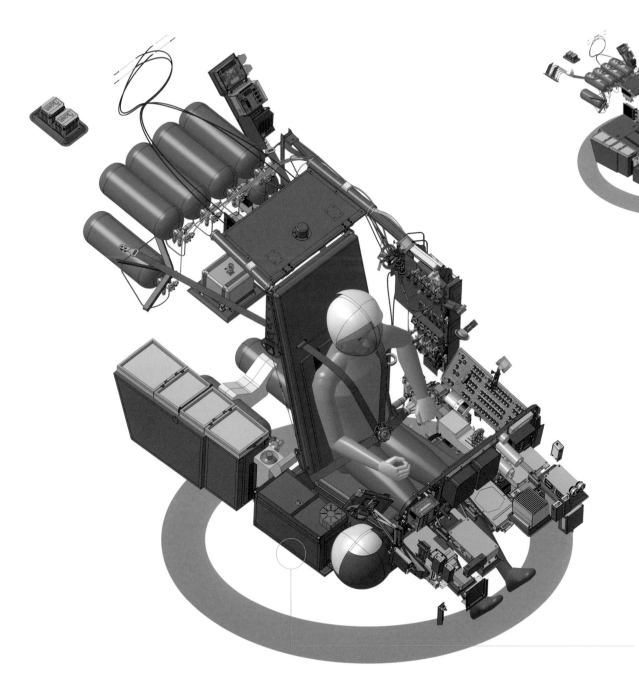

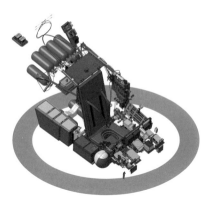

### Lantal
A multi-purpose inflatable seat serving as both a reclining couchette and a toilet.

### Altran
Tailor-made auto-pilot incorporating a monitoring system which alerts the pilot during rest periods if safety parameters are exceeded.

### Omega
An on-board instrument to indicate the bank angle with a precision of one degree.

### Air Liquide
Pilot oxygen life support.

### Nestlé Health Science
Specially packaged meals for extreme temperatures.

### Swisscom
A very low consumption telecommunications system that transmits data by telemetry to Mission Control Center, and a low-bandwidth solution for broadcasting live pictures of the pilot.

### Google
Google hangouts to connect with and inspire young net surfers and help raise global awareness of renewable energy use.

### EPFL
A feasibility study that gave the project credibility from the very beginning. Scientific advisor on many developments.

### Dassault Systèmes
3D design software.

# PATRONS | PARRAINS | PATEN

SIR RICHARD BRANSON

JOSEPH ACKERMANN
BUZZ ALDRIN
YANN ARTHUS-BERTRAND
SIR RICHARD BRANSON
JAMES CAMERON
PAULO COELHO

HSH ALBERT II DE MONACO
PETER DIAMANDIS
JEAN-LOUIS ETIENNE
AL GORE
NICOLAS HULOT
ERIK LINDBERGH

HUBERT REEVES
ROBERT SWAN
JEAN VERNE
DON WALSH
RICHARD WIESE
ELIE WIESEL

AL GORE

ERIK LINDBERGH

ELIE WIESEL

DON WALSH AND JAMES CAMERON

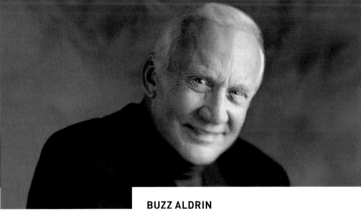

BUZZ ALDRIN

YANN ARTHUS-BERTRAND

HUBERT REEVES

HSH ALBERT II DE MONACO

PAULO COELHO

# **SUPPORTERS** | **SUPPORTERS** | SUPPORTER

**Each supporter knows that his or her name will travel around the world in the airplane's cockpit.**

**Chaque supporter sait que son nom voyagera dans le cockpit de l'avion du tour du monde.**

Jeder Supporter weiß, dass sein Name im Cockpit des Round-the-World-Flugzeugs mitfliegt.

**AT EVERY LANDING, CROWDS FASCINATED TO SEE HISTORY BEING MADE BEFORE THEIR VERY EYES.**

À CHAQUE ATTERRISSAGE, UNE FOULE FASCINÉE DE VOIR UNE PAGE DE L'HISTOIRE SE DÉROULER DEVANT SES YEUX.

BEI JEDER LANDUNG VERSAMMELT SICH EINE BEGEISTERTE MENGE, DIE MIT EIGENEN AUGEN ZUSIEHT, WIE EIN NEUES KAPITEL DER GESCHICHTE GESCHRIEBEN WIRD.

## THE MISSIONS
## LES MISSIONS
## DIE MISSIONSFLÜGE

## FLIGHT LOG

8 WORLD RECORDS FOR THE PROTOTYPE
SOLAR IMPULSE 1, FROM THE 1st NIGHT
FLIGHT OF A SOLAR AIRPLANE TO ITS
MISSION FLIGHTS.

In Europe, in North Africa and in
America, to share a vision of the
future with the public and politicians,
as a prelude to going round the world.

## UN CARNET DE VOLS

8 RECORDS DU MONDE POUR
LE PROTOTYPE SOLAR IMPULSE 1,
DU 1er VOL DE NUIT D'UN AVION
SOLAIRE AUX VOLS DE MISSION.

En Europe, en Afrique du Nord et en
Amérique, pour partager une vision
du futur avec le public et le monde
politique, en prélude au tour du monde.

## EIN LOGBUCH

8 WELTREKORDE FÜR DEN PROTOTYP
SOLAR IMPULSE 1, VOM ERSTEN
NACHTFLUG EINES SOLARFLUGZEUGS
BIS ZU DEN MISSIONSFLÜGEN.

Während der Flüge über Europa,
Nordafrika und die USA wird im Vorfeld
der Weltumrundung eine Vision für die
Zukunft mit der Öffentlichkeit und politi-
schen Entscheidungsträgern geteilt.

# 2010 | NIGHT FLIGHT

## WESTERN SWITZERLAND

**PILOT**
André Borschberg

**TAKE-OFF TIME**
07.07.2010 / 06:51 AM
(local time)

**LANDING TIME**
08.07.2010 / 09:02 AM
(local time)

**FLIGHT DURATION**
26 h, 10 min, 19 sec

**FAI WORLD RECORDS**
André Borschberg

Duration
26 h, 10 min, 19 sec

Absolute altitude
9,235 m / 30,000 ft

Gain of height
8,744 m / 28,688 ft

PAYERNE

07–
08

Payerne region
← 06:51 AM
→ 09:02 AM

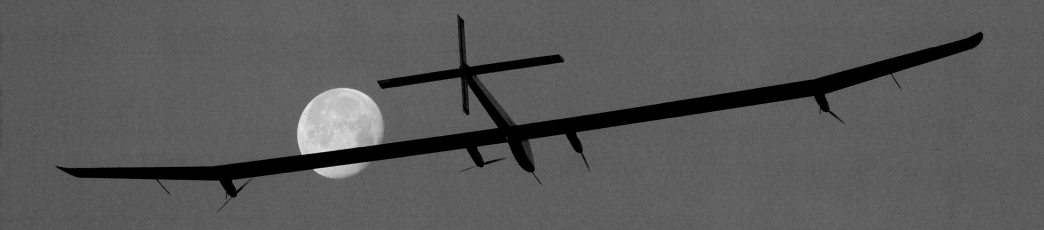

## WILL THE PLANE SEE DAY BREAK BEFORE ITS BATTERIES RUN OUT?

L'AVION ATTEINDRA-T-IL LE LEVER DU JOUR AVANT QUE SES BATTERIES NE SOIENT VIDES ?

SCHAFFT ES DAS FLUGZEUG BIS ZUM SONNENAUFGANG, BEVOR SEINE BATTERIEN LEER SIND ?

**IT CAN BE DONE! AN AIRCRAFT CAN FLY DAY AND NIGHT WITHOUT FUEL. A HISTORIC FIRST!**

LA DÉMONSTRATION EST FAITE: UN AVION PEUT VOLER JOUR ET NUIT SANS CARBURANT. UNE PREMIÈRE HISTORIQUE!

DER BEWEIS IST ERBRACHT: EIN FLUGZEUG KANN TAG UND NACHT OHNE TREIBSTOFF FLIEGEN. EINE HISTORISCHE PREMIERE!

# 2010–2012 | **SWISS FLIGHTS**

AROUND THE WORLD IN A SOLAR AIRPLANE
SOLAR**IMPULSE**
HB-SIA

| **PAYERNE – GENEVA** | **PAYERNE – ZURICH** | **MATTERHORN** |
|---|---|---|
| PILOT<br>André Borschberg | PILOT<br>André Borschberg | PILOT<br>Bertrand Piccard |
| TAKE-OFF TIME<br>21.09.2010 / 08:04 AM<br>(local time) | TAKE-OFF TIME<br>22.09.2010 / 08:09 AM<br>(local time) | TAKE-OFF TIME<br>07.05.2012 / 04:14 AM<br>(local time) |
| LANDING TIME<br>21.09.2010 / 12:24 PM<br>(local time) | LANDING TIME<br>22.09.2010 / 02:30 PM<br>(local time) | LANDING TIME<br>07.05.2012 / 10:51 PM<br>(local time) |
| FLIGHT<br>DURATION<br>4h, 20min | FLIGHT<br>DURATION<br>6h, 21min | FLIGHT<br>DURATION<br>18h, 37min |

**TOTAL FLIGHTS
IN 2010**
**17**

**TOTAL FLIGHT
TIME**
**80h, 17min**

ZURICH
PAYERNE
GENEVA
MATTERHORN

**21 22**

| Payerne –<br>Geneva | Payerne –<br>Zurich |
|---|---|
| → 08:04 AM | → 08:09 AM |
| ← 12:24 PM | ← 02:30 PM |

**AN IDEA BORN IN SWITZERLAND:
CUTTING EDGE TECHNOLOGY,
INNOVATION AND KNOW-HOW.**

**UNE IDÉE NÉE EN SUISSE:
TECHNOLOGIE DE POINTE,
INNOVATION ET SAVOIR-FAIRE.**

EINE IDEE AUS DER SCHWEIZ:
SPITZENTECHNOLOGIE,
INNOVATION UND KNOW-HOW.

**07**

Matterhorn
→ 04:14 AM
← 10:51 PM

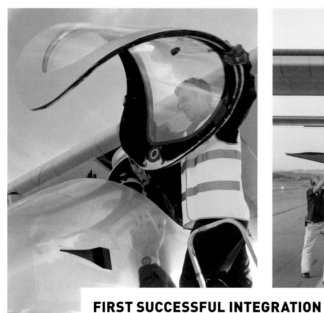

**FIRST SUCCESSFUL INTEGRATION IN AIR TRAFFIC OF SUCH A SLOW AIRCRAFT. IMAGINE A PEDESTRIAN ON A FREEWAY!**

**PREMIÈRE INTÉGRATION RÉUSSIE D'UN AVION AUSSI LENT DANS LE TRAFIC AÉRIEN. IMAGINEZ UN PIÉTON SUR UNE AUTOROUTE!**

DIE ERSTE ERFOLGREICHE INTEGRATION EINES ULTRA-LANGSAMEN FLUGZEUGS IN DEN FLUGVERKEHR. MAN STELLE SICH NUR EINEN FUSSGÄNGER AUF DER AUTOBAHN VOR!

# 2011 | EUROPEAN FLIGHTS

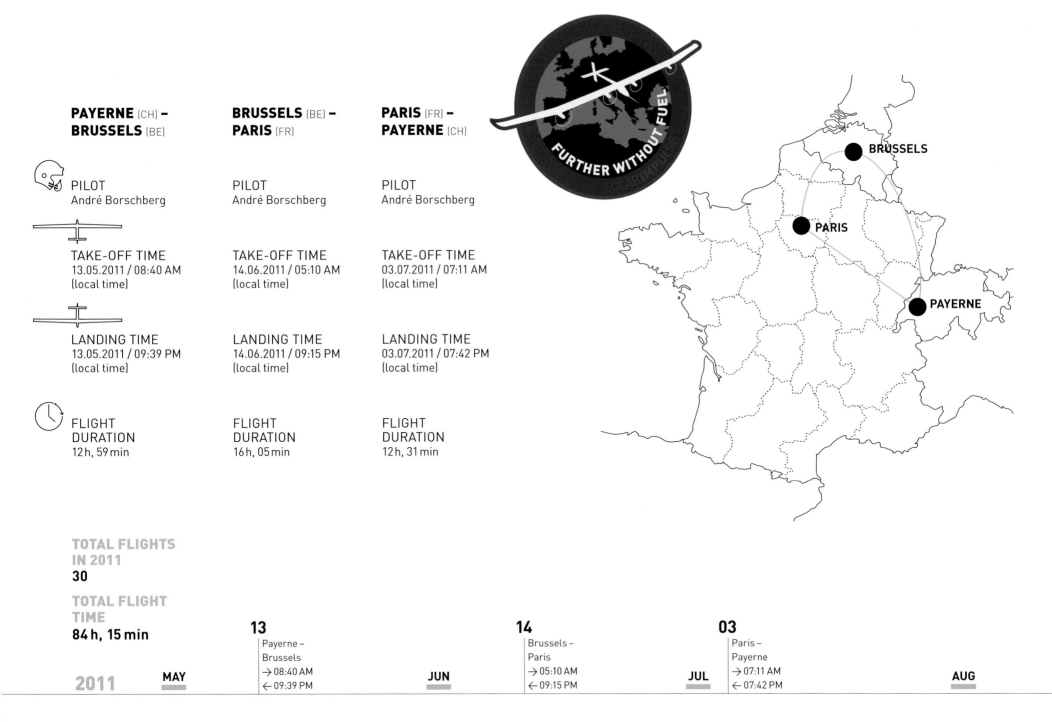

**PAYERNE** (CH) **–**
**BRUSSELS** (BE)

PILOT
André Borschberg

TAKE-OFF TIME
13.05.2011 / 08:40 AM
(local time)

LANDING TIME
13.05.2011 / 09:39 PM
(local time)

FLIGHT
DURATION
12h, 59min

**BRUSSELS** (BE) **–**
**PARIS** (FR)

PILOT
André Borschberg

TAKE-OFF TIME
14.06.2011 / 05:10 AM
(local time)

LANDING TIME
14.06.2011 / 09:15 PM
(local time)

FLIGHT
DURATION
16h, 05min

**PARIS** (FR) **–**
**PAYERNE** (CH)

PILOT
André Borschberg

TAKE-OFF TIME
03.07.2011 / 07:11 AM
(local time)

LANDING TIME
03.07.2011 / 07:42 PM
(local time)

FLIGHT
DURATION
12h, 31min

**TOTAL FLIGHTS
IN 2011
30**

**TOTAL FLIGHT
TIME
84h, 15min**

**2011**

MAY

**13**
Payerne –
Brussels
→ 08:40 AM
← 09:39 PM

JUN

**14**
Brussels –
Paris
→ 05:10 AM
← 09:15 PM

JUL

**03**
Paris –
Payerne
→ 07:11 AM
← 07:42 PM

AUG

**A ROYAL WELCOME IN BRUSSELS AND PATRONAGE FROM THE EUROPEAN COMMUNITY.**

ACCUEIL ROYAL À BRUXELLES ET PARRAINAGE DE LA COMMUNAUTÉ EUROPÉENNE.

FÜRSTLICHER EMPFANG IN BRÜSSEL UND PATENSCHAFT DER EUROPÄISCHEN GEMEINSCHAFT.

**CHANGES IN ENERGY POLICY WILL ONLY HAPPEN IF THE PUBLIC AND THE MEDIA SHOW MORE SUPPORT.**

DES CHANGEMENTS DE POLITIQUE ÉNERGÉTIQUE NE DEVIENDRONT RÉALITÉ QU'AVEC UN SOUTIEN ACCRU DU PUBLIC ET DES MÉDIAS.

ÄNDERUNGEN IN DER ENERGIE-POLITIK WERDEN NUR MIT EINER DEUTLICHEN UNTERSTÜTZUNG VON SEITEN DER ÖFFENTLICHKEIT UND DER MEDIEN ERFOLGEN.

**GUEST OF HONOR AT THE PARIS-LE BOURGET AIR SHOW, SOLAR IMPULSE SHOWS THE WAY IN INNOVATION!**

INVITÉ D'HONNEUR AU SALON AÉRONAUTIQUE DU BOURGET, SOLAR IMPULSE MONTRE LA VOIE DE L'INNOVATION!

ALS EHRENGAST BEI DER LUFTFAHRTSCHAU IN PARIS-LE BOURGET ZEIGT SOLAR IMPULSE DEN WEG DER INNOVATION!

**ON THE GROUND AS WELL, THE IMPOSSIBLE COULD BE ACHIEVED WITH RENEWABLE ENERGY.**

AU SOL AUSSI, ON PEUT ACCOMPLIR L'IMPOSSIBLE AVEC DES ÉNERGIES RENOUVELABLES.

AUCH AM BODEN KÖNNTE MAN MIT ERNEUERBAREN ENERGIEN DAS UNMÖGLICHE MÖGLICH MACHEN.

**CLEAN TECHNOLOGIES CREATE JOBS AND GROWTH.**

LES TECHNOLOGIES PROPRES SONT CRÉATRICES D'EMPLOIS ET DE CROISSANCE.

SAUBERE TECHNOLOGIEN SORGEN FÜR ARBEITSPLÄTZE UND WACHSTUM.

# 2012 | INTERCONTINENTAL FLIGHTS

**PAYERNE** (CH) **– MADRID** (ES)
**MADRID** (ES) **– RABAT** (MA)
**RABAT** (MA) **– OUARZAZATE** (MA)
**OUARZAZATE** (MA) **– RABAT** (MA)
**RABAT** (MA) **– MADRID** (ES)
**MADRID** (ES) **– TOULOUSE** (FR)
**TOULOUSE** (FR) **– PAYERNE** (CH)

PILOT
André Borschberg
Bertrand Piccard

7 FLIGHTS

FLIGHT
TIME
115h, 5min

FAI WORLD
RECORDS
André Borschberg

Free distance
along a course
1,116km / 693miles

Straight distance
1,099.3km / 683miles

**TOTAL FLIGHTS
IN 2012
17**

**TOTAL FLIGHT
TIME
181 h, 48 min**

**2012**     MAY

| 24–25 | | 05 | | 21–22 | 29 | | 06–07 | | 17 | | 24 | |
|---|---|---|---|---|---|---|---|---|---|---|---|---|
| Payerne – Madrid | | Madrid – Rabat | | Rabat – Ouarzazate | Ouarzazate – Rabat | | Rabat – Madrid | | Madrid – Toulouse | | Toulouse – Payerne | |
| → 08:24 AM | | → 05:22 AM | | → 07:05 AM | → 07:33 AM | | → 06:17 AM | | → 05:33 AM | | → 07:01 AM | |
| ← 01:28 AM | JUN | ← 11:30 PM | | ← 00:25 AM | ← 10:22 PM | JUL | ← 01:19 AM | | ← 09:46 PM | | ← 08:30 PM | AUG |

**FOLLOWING IN THE FOOTSTEPS OF THE PIONEERS OF THE "AEROPOSTALE".**

SUR LES TRACES DES PIONNIERS DE L'AÉROPOSTALE.

AUF DEN SPUREN DER LUFTPOSTPIONIERE.

**PILOTS DECORATED BY KING MOHAMMED VI FOR THEIR SUPPORT OF THE MOROCCAN SOLAR PROGRAM.**

PILOTES DÉCORÉS PAR LE ROI MOHAMMED VI POUR LEUR SOUTIEN AU PROGRAMME SOLAIRE MAROCAIN.

AUSZEICHNUNG DER PILOTEN DURCH KÖNIG MOHAMMED VI FÜR IHRE UNTERSTÜTZUNG DES MAROKKANI- SCHEN SOLARPROGRAMMS.

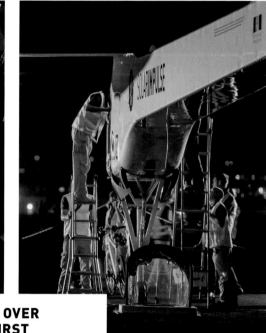

**EXCITEMENT IN RABAT OVER THE ARRIVAL OF THE FIRST INTERCONTINENTAL FLIGHT OF A SOLAR AIRPLANE.**

EFFERVESCENCE À RABAT POUR L'ARRIVÉE DU PREMIER VOL INTERCONTINENTAL D'UN AVION SOLAIRE.

BEGEISTERUNG IN RABAT BEI DER ANKUNFT DES ERSTEN INTERKONTINENTALFLUGS EINES SOLARFLUGZEUGS.

# 2013 | ACROSS AMERICA FLIGHTS

**MOFFETT AIRFIELD – PHOENIX** (CA)
**PHOENIX – DALLAS** (AZ)
**DALLAS – ST. LOUIS** (TX)
**ST. LOUIS – CINCINNATI** (OH)
**CINCINNATI – WASHINGTON D.C.** (DC)
**WASHINGTON D.C. – NEW YORK** (NY)

**PILOT**
André Borschberg
Bertrand Piccard

**6 FLIGHTS**

**FLIGHT TIME**
105 h, 41 min

**FAI WORLD
RECORDS**
André Borschberg

Free distance
1,506.5 km / 936 miles

Straight distance
1,386.5 km / 861.5 miles

Free distance
along a course
1,487.6 km / 924 miles

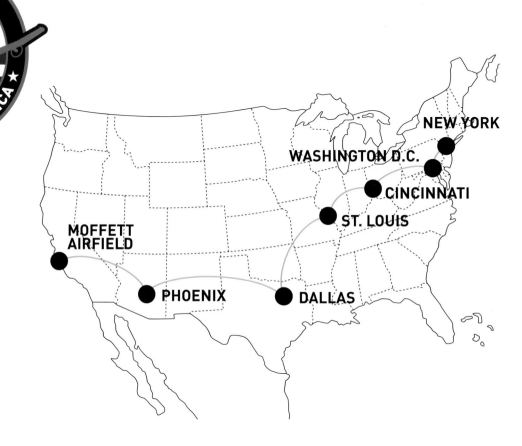

**TOTAL FLIGHTS
IN 2013**
13

**TOTAL FLIGHT
TIME**
127 h, 23 min

**2013**

| | MAY | | JUN | | | | JUL | | AUG |
|---|---|---|---|---|---|---|---|---|---|
| | **03–04** | | **22–23** | | **03–04** | **14** | **15–16** | **06** | |
| | Moffett Airfield –<br>Phoenix | | Phoenix –<br>Dallas | | Dallas –<br>St. Louis | St. Louis –<br>Cincinnati | Cincinnati –<br>Washington D.C. | Washington D.C. –<br>New York | |
| | → 06:12 AM | | → 04:47 AM | | → 04:06 AM | → 04:01 AM | → 10:11 AM | → 04:46 AM | |
| | ← 00:30 AM | | ← 01:08 AM | | ← 01:28 AM | ← 08:15 PM | ← 00:15 AM | ← 11:09 AM | |

**6 STAGES BETWEEN SAN FRANCISCO AND NEW YORK. FINAL PREPARATIONS BEFORE THE ROUND-THE-WORLD TRIP.**

**6 ÉTAPES ENTRE SAN FRANCISCO ET NEW YORK. DERNIERS ENTRAÎNEMENTS AVANT LE TOUR DU MONDE.**

6 ETAPPEN ZWISCHEN SAN FRANCISCO UND NEW YORK. LETZTE TRAININGS VOR DER WELTUMRUNDUNG.

**3,500 MILES OF AWESOME
FLIGHTS DESPITE UNFORESEEN
METEOROLOGICAL, TECHNICAL
AND OPERATIONAL SNAGS.**

5650 KILOMÈTRES DE VOLS À COUPER
LE SOUFFLE MALGRÉ LES IMPRÉVUS
MÉTÉOROLOGIQUES, TECHNIQUES
ET OPÉRATIONNELS.

5650 ATEMBERAUBENDE FLUGKILO-
METER TROTZ UNVORHERSEHBARER
METEOROLOGISCHER, TECHNISCHER
UND OPERATIVER EREIGNISSE.

**THE AMERICAN DREAM IN
THE COUNTRY OF THE PIONEERS:
8.5 BILLION MEDIA HITS.**

LE RÊVE AMÉRICAIN AU PAYS
DES PIONNIERS: 8,5 MILLIARDS
DE RETOMBÉES MÉDIAS.

DER AMERIKANISCHE TRAUM
IM LAND DER PIONIERE MIT EINER
MEDIENRESONANZ VON 8,5 MRD.
BEITRÄGEN.

**NEW YORK IN SIGHT, AN EXPERI-
MENTAL PROTOTYPE AT ONE OF
THE WORLD'S LARGEST AIRPORTS.**

NEW YORK EN VUE, UN PROTOTYPE
EXPÉRIMENTAL SUR UN DES PLUS
GRANDS AÉROPORTS DU MONDE.

NEW YORK VORAUS. EIN EXPERIMEN-
TELLER PROTOTYP AUF EINEM DER
GRÖSSTEN FLUGHÄFEN DER WELT.

**MANKIND COULD HALVE ENERGY CONSUMPTION BY REPLACING OLD TECHNOLOGIES WITH CLEAN TECHS.**

**L'HUMANITÉ POURRAIT DIVISER PAR DEUX SA CONSOMMATION ÉNERGÉTIQUE EN REMPLAÇANT LES VIEILLES TECHNOLOGIES PAR DES TECHNOLOGIES PROPRES.**

DIE MENSCHHEIT KÖNNTE IHREN ENERGIEVERBRAUCH HALBIEREN, INDEM SIE ALTE TECHNOLOGIEN MIT SAUBEREN TECHNOLOGIEN ERSETZT.

**A POWERFUL MESSAGE THAT
RESONATES WITH THE UN's
ENVIRONMENTAL POLICY.**

UN MESSAGE FORT QUI CONVERGE
AVEC LA POLITIQUE ENVIRON-
NEMENTALE DES NATIONS UNIES.

EINE STARKE BOTSCHAFT IM
EINKLANG MIT DER UMWELTPOLITIK
DER VEREINTEN NATIONEN.

**A CHALLENGE**
UN CHALLENGE
EINE HERAUSFORDERUNG

MLG Dynam
#1 (Pre-T
June-27-2013

## TECHNICAL CHALLENGE

TO TAKE AN AIRPLANE TO SUCH A HIGH LEVEL OF ENERGY EFFICIENCY THAT IT CAN FLY DAY AND NIGHT RELYING ONLY ON THE SUN.

What major civil and military aircraft makers thought impossible has been achieved by the ingenuity of a small team.

## CHALLENGE TECHNIQUE

PORTER L'AVION À UN TEL DEGRÉ D'EFFICIENCE ÉNERGÉTIQUE QU'IL PUISSE SE CONTENTER DU SOLEIL POUR VOLER JOUR ET NUIT.

Ce que les grands constructeurs aéronautiques civils et militaires ont jugé impossible a été réalisé par une petite équipe ingénieuse.

## TECHNISCHE HERAUS-FORDERUNG

EINE ENERGIEEFFIZIENZ ERREICHEN, MIT DER DAS FLUGZEUG ALLEIN MIT DER KRAFT DER SONNE TAG UND NACHT FLIEGEN KANN.

Die großen Konstrukteure der Zivil- und Militärluftfahrt haben es für unmöglich gehalten. Ein kleines Ingenieursteam hat es möglich gemacht.

**An extraordinary feat by engineers: cutting every possible ounce of weight from the structure to get more batteries on board.**

Prouesse des ingénieurs qui ont économisé chaque gramme sur la structure pour pouvoir embarquer davantage de batteries.

Eine technische Meisterleistung, bei der die Ingenieure jedes Gramm bei der Struktur des Flugzeugs eingespart haben, um ein Maximum an Batterieleistung mit an Bord nehmen zu können.

**The components normally used in aircraft construction are far too heavy for Solar Impulse.**

Impossible de recourir aux composants normalement utilisés dans l'aéronautique – ils sont trop lourds.

Es ist unmöglich, auf normale Verbundmaterialien der Luftfahrt zurückzugreifen. Sie sind zu schwer.

**JOINING FORCES, FROM DRAWING-BOARD TO AIRFRAME CONSTRUCTION, TO TURN A VISION INTO REALITY.**

**UNIR DES FORCES, DU DESIGN À LA CONSTRUCTION DE LA STRUCTURE, ET FAIRE D'UNE VISION UNE RÉALITÉ.**

KRÄFTE BÜNDELN, VOM DESIGN BIS ZUR KONSTRUKTION DES FLUGZEUGS. SO WIRD AUS EINER VISION WIRKLICHKEIT.

**INNOVATING, CONSTANTLY IMPROVING, AND FINDING NEW PRODUCTS WITH TECHNICAL PARTNERS.**

INNOVER, SE SURPASSER ET DÉBOUCHER SUR DE NOUVEAUX PRODUITS EN COLLABORATION AVEC DES PARTENAIRES TECHNIQUES.

IN ZUSAMMENARBEIT MIT DEN TECHNISCHEN PARTNERN INNOVATIONEN EINFÜHREN, ÜBER SICH HINAUS WACHSEN UND NEUE PRODUKTDESIGNS ENTWERFEN.

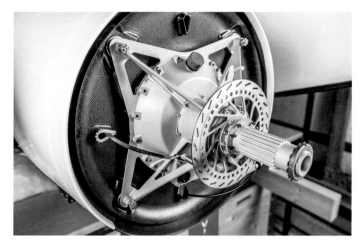

**A record 97 % efficiency from the four 17.4 HP motors.**

Un rendement record de 97 % pour les quatre
moteurs de 17,4 CV.

Eine rekordverdächtige Effizienz von 97 % für die vier,
je 17,4 PS starken Motoren.

**THE SOLAR PANELS ARE FIXED DIRECTLY TO THE INTERNAL FRAME OF THE WING.**

LES PANNEAUX SOLAIRES SONT DIRECTEMENT FIXÉS SUR LA STRUCTURE INTÉRIEURE DE L'AILE.

DIE SOLARPANELS WERDEN DIREKT AN DER INNENSTRUKTUR DER TRAGFLÄCHE BEFESTIGT.

**140 carbon fiber ribs spaced at 50 centimeter (19 ¾ inch) intervals give the wing its aerodynamic shape while providing rigidity.**

140 nervures en fibre de carbone réparties tous les 50 cm donnent à l'aile son profil aérodynamique tout en garantissant sa rigidité.

140, im Abstand von jeweils 50 Zentimetern angebrachte Karbonfaserrippen geben der Tragfläche ihre aerodynamische und widerstandsfähige Form.

**If a solar airplane can fly, imagine what could be done in our society with the same technologies.**

Si un avion solaire peut voler, imaginez tout ce qu'il serait possible de faire dans notre société avec les mêmes technologies.

Wenn ein Solarflugzeug fliegen kann, stellen Sie sich vor, was sonst noch mit denselben Technologien erreicht werden kann.

**A honeycomb sandwich assembly and layers of carbon fiber 3 times lighter than a sheet of paper (0.74 oz/yd²).**

Assemblage en sandwich de nid d'abeilles et de couches de fibres de carbone 3 fois plus légères qu'une feuille de papier (25 g/m²).

Konstruktion aus einer wabenartigen Sandwichstruktur mit Karbonfaserschichten, die dreimal leichter sind als ein Blatt Papier (25 g/m²).

**THE LARGEST AIRPLANE EVER BUILT WEIGHING SO LITTLE.**

LE PLUS GRAND AVION JAMAIS CONSTRUIT POUR UN POIDS AUSSI FAIBLE.

DAS GRÖSSTE UND GLEICHZEITIG LEICHTESTE FLUGZEUG, DAS JE GEBAUT WURDE.

**With no heating, the pilot and the batteries are protected from the minus 40 degrees outside temperature by high density foam insulation.**

En l'absence de chauffage, le pilote et les batteries sont protégés des -40 degrés extérieurs par une isolation en mousse de haute densité.

Der Pilot und die Batterien sind wegen der fehlenden Heizung durch einen hochdichten Isolationsschaum gegen Außentemperaturen von -40 Grad geschützt.

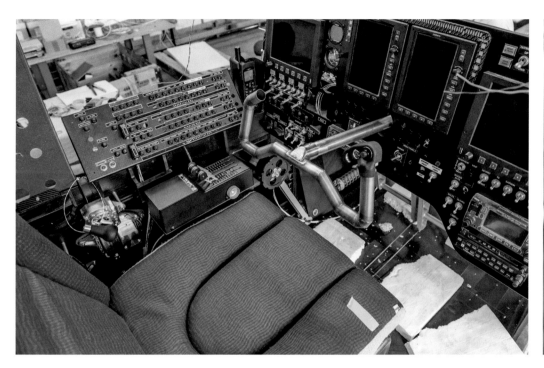

**A multi-purpose seat serves as both a reclining berth and a toilet. A parachute and a life raft are packed into the seat back.**

Un siège polyvalent sert à la fois de couchette et de toilette. Un parachute et un canot de sauvetage sont intégrés dans le dossier.

Ein Multifunktionssitz, der gleichzeitig als Schlafkoje und als Toilette dient. In der Rückenlehne sind ein Fallschirm und ein Rettungsboot integriert.

**Most instruments on board have been specially designed by the team of electricians.**

La plupart des instruments de bord ont été conçus spécialement par l'équipe des électriciens.

Die meisten Bordinstrumente sind eine Sonderanfertigung des Elektrotechnik-Teams.

**CLOSE ENCOUNTER OF THE 3RD KIND IN A WIND TUNNEL TEST.**

RENCONTRE DU 3e TYPE POUR UN TEST EN SOUFFLERIE.

EINE BEGEGNUNG DER 3. ART FÜR EINEN TEST IM WINDKANAL.

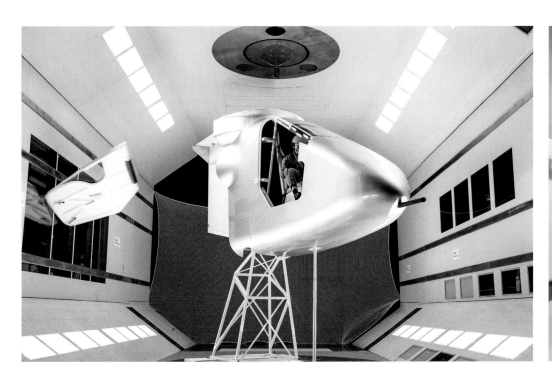

**The door can be jettisoned if the pilot has to make a parachute jump.**

La porte peut être larguée si le pilote doit sauter en parachute.

Die Tür kann abgekoppelt werden, falls der Pilot mit dem Fallschirm abspringen muss.

**Energy efficiency is also achieved through aerodynamic performance.**

L'efficience énergétique passe aussi par la performance aérodynamique.

Die Energieeffizienz wird auch durch die aerodynamische Leistung beeinflusst.

**The 17,248 solar cells of monocrystalline silicon 135 microns thick are the best compromise between lightness, flexibility and efficiency (23 %).**

Les 17 248 cellules solaires en silicium monocrystallin de 135 microns présentent le meilleur compromis entre légèreté, flexibilité et rendement (23 %).

Die 17 248 Solarzellen sind aus 135 Mikrometer dünnem, monokristallinem Silizium und bilden den optimalen Kompromiss zwischen Leichtigkeit, Flexibilität und Wirkungsgrad (23 %).

## ENERGY OF THE FUTURE ON THE WINGS, FUSELAGE AND PLANE'S TAIL.

## L'ÉNERGIE DU FUTUR SUR LES AILES, LE FUSELAGE ET L'EMPENNAGE.

### DIE ENERGIE DER ZUKUNFT AUF TRAGFLÄCHE, RUMPF UND LEITWERK.

**A new encapsulation method had to be invented to protect the solar panels.**

Un nouveau mode d'encapsulation a dû être inventé pour protéger les panneaux solaires.

Erfindung einer neuartigen Verkapselungstechnik zum Schutz der Solarpanels.

**THE WING SPAN OF A BOEING 747 JUMBO JET 236 FEET. THE WEIGHT OF A FAMILY CAR 5,000 LBS. THE POWER OF A SMALL MOTORCYCLE 70 HP.**

L'ENVERGURE D'UN BOEING 747 JUMBO JET 72 MÈTRES. LE POIDS D'UNE VOITURE FAMILIALE 2300 KG. LA PUISSANCE D'UNE MOTO 70 CV.

SPANNWEITE EINER BOEING 747 (JUMBO JET) 72 METER. GEWICHT EINES PKW 2300 KG. LEISTUNG EINES MOTORRADS 70 PS.

**All scientific breakthroughs start with a crazy idea.
First it's said to be impossible, then it becomes
a reality and finally it appears self-evident.**

Toute conquête scientifique commence par
une idée folle. Au début, on la dit impossible.
Puis, elle devient réalité, avant d'aller de soi.

Jede wissenschaftliche Errungenschaft beginnt
mit einer verrückten Idee. Am Anfang gilt sie
als unmöglich. Dann setzt man sie um, bevor sie
zu einer Selbstverständlichkeit wird.

———

**Markus Scherdel at work: the airplane must
be certified by a qualified test pilot.**

**Markus Scherdel à l'oeuvre: l'avion doit être
certifié par un pilote d'essai professionnel.**

Markus Scherdel bei der Arbeit: Das Flugzeug
muss von einem professionellen Testpiloten
zertifiziert werden.

**"A GIANT STEP FORWARD,
SENDING A STRONG MESSAGE TO
PEOPLE AROUND THE WORLD."**
Ban Ki-moon (UN Secretary-General)

**"UN PAS DE GÉANT ADRESSANT UN
MESSAGE FORT AU MONDE ENTIER."**
Ban Ki-moon (secrétaire général de l'ONU)

"EIN ENORMER SCHRITT NACH VORNE
MIT EINER STARKEN BOTSCHAFT
AN ALLE MENSCHEN DIESER WELT."
Ban Ki-moon (Generalsekretär der Vereinten Nationen)

## HUMAN CHALLENGE

THE CHALLENGE IS ENORMOUS.
TO CROSS THE OCEANS THE PLANE
MUST FLY FOR 5 CONSECUTIVE
DAYS AND NIGHTS.

In a non-pressurized unheated cockpit,
the pilot must have exceptional stamina
to control this plane which is sensitive
to turbulence because of its broad wing
span and light weight.

## CHALLENGE HUMAIN

LE DÉFI EST EXTRÊME. IL FAUDRA VOLER
JUSQU'À 5 JOURS ET 5 NUITS D'AFFILÉE
POUR TRAVERSER LES OCÉANS.

Dans un cockpit non pressurisé et non
chauffé, le pilote devra faire preuve d'une
endurance hors normes pour contrôler
cet avion que son envergure et sa
légèreté rendent sensible aux turbulences.

## MENSCHLICHE HERAUS-FORDERUNG

EINE EXTREME HERAUSFORDERUNG.
DIE ÜBERQUERUNG DER OZEANE
DAUERT BIS ZU 5 TAGE UND NÄCHTE.

In einem unbeheizten Cockpit ohne
Druckkabine muss der Pilot über ein
beachtliches Durchhaltevermögen
verfügen, um das Flugzeug zu steuern,
das durch seine Spannweite und
Leichtigkeit anfällig für Turbulenzen ist.

**THE AIRCRAFT'S ENDURANCE IS UNLIMITED. HOW CAN WE INCREASE THE PILOT'S ENDURANCE?**

**L'AUTONOMIE DE L'AVION EST ILLIMITÉE. COMMENT AUGMENTER CELLE DU PILOTE?**

DIE AUTONOMIE DES FLUGZEUGS IST UNBEGRENZT. WIE KANN MAN DIE AUTONOMIE DES PILOTEN ERHÖHEN?

**In the flight simulator the pilots can practice the airplane's delicate maneuvers on long missions.**

Un simulateur de vol pour entraîner les pilotes au maniement délicat de l'avion sur de longues missions.

Mit einem Flugsimulator können sich die Piloten auf die empfindliche Steuerung ihres Flugzeugs während der Langstreckenflüge vorbereiten.

**YOGA AND MEDITATION TECHNIQUES TO MAINTAIN POWERS OF CONCENTRATION.**

YOGA ET TECHNIQUES DE MÉDITATION POUR CONSERVER SES FACULTÉS DE CONCENTRATION.

YOGA UND MEDITATIONSTECHNIKEN DIENEN DAZU, DIE KONZENTRATIONS-FÄHIGKEIT AUFRECHT ZU ERHALTEN.

**SELF-HYPNOSIS FOR FATIGUE MANAGEMENT IN 10 SESSIONS OF 20 MINUTES PER DAY.**

AUTOHYPNOSE, POUR SE RÉGÉNÉRER PAR SÉANCE DE 20 MINUTES, 10 FOIS PAR JOUR.

SELBSTHYPNOSE ZUR REGENERATION IN JEWEILS 20-MINUTEN-SEQUENZEN, 10 MAL AM TAG.

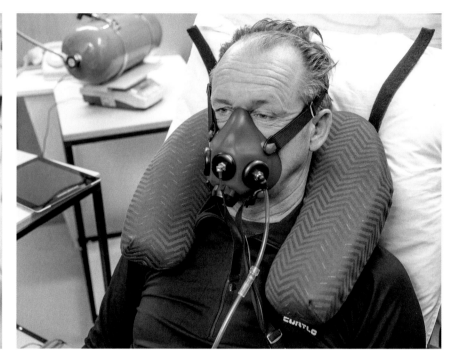

**In a decompression chamber, practice in vigilance tests to be done 4 times a day.**

En chambre de décompression, entraînement des tests de vigilance qui seront effectués 4x/jour.

4 Mal täglich Trainingseinheiten zur Überprüfung des Wachsamkeitsniveaus in der Dekompressionskammer.

**12 hours per day in an oxygen mask above 12,000 feet.**

12 heures par jour sous masque à oxygène au-dessus de 3600 mètres.

12 Stunden täglich mit einer Sauerstoffmaske über einer Flughöhe von 3600 Meter.

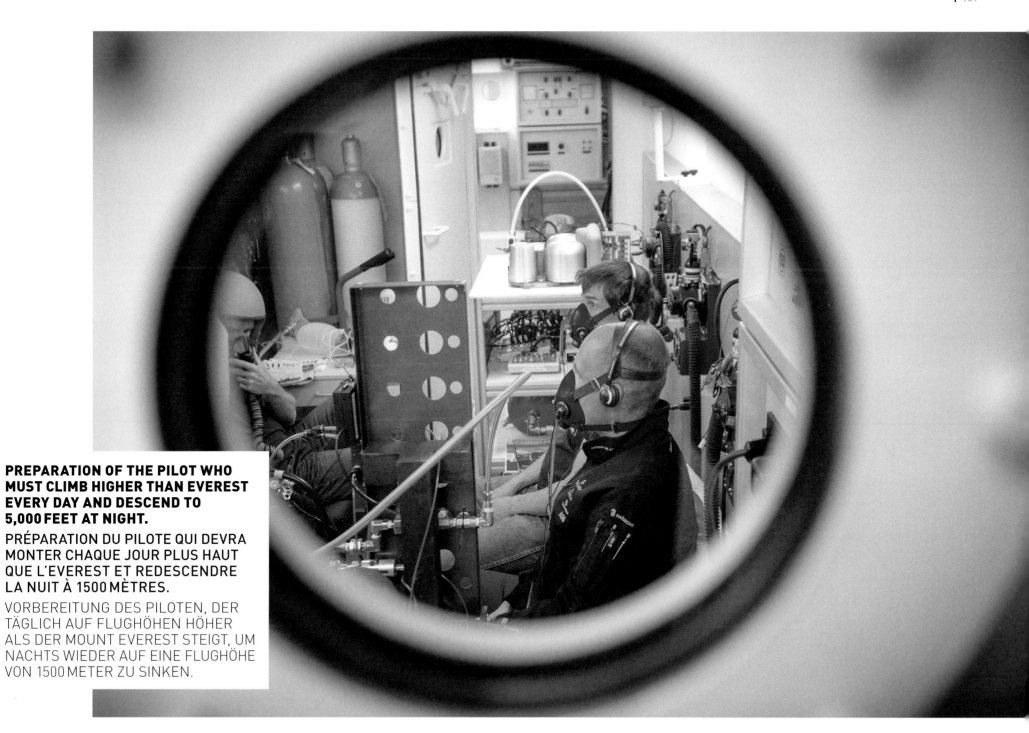

**PREPARATION OF THE PILOT WHO MUST CLIMB HIGHER THAN EVEREST EVERY DAY AND DESCEND TO 5,000 FEET AT NIGHT.**

PRÉPARATION DU PILOTE QUI DEVRA MONTER CHAQUE JOUR PLUS HAUT QUE L'EVEREST ET REDESCENDRE LA NUIT À 1500 MÈTRES.

VORBEREITUNG DES PILOTEN, DER TÄGLICH AUF FLUGHÖHEN HÖHER ALS DER MOUNT EVEREST STEIGT, UM NACHTS WIEDER AUF EINE FLUGHÖHE VON 1500 METER ZU SINKEN.

**"FLYING HAS ALWAYS BEEN THE GREAT PASSION OF MY LIFE...**

"VOLER EST DEPUIS TOUJOURS LA GRANDE PASSION DE MA VIE...

"FLIEGEN WAR SCHON IMMER MEINE GROSSE LEIDENSCHAFT...

**...it taught me to anticipate, to think in the future. That ability also comes in useful in my life as an entrepreneur."**

...j'y ai appris à anticiper, penser dans le futur. C'est une aptitude que j'utilise aussi dans ma vie d'entrepreneur."

...dabei habe ich gelernt, vorausschauend zu agieren und in der Zukunft zu denken. Diese Fähigkeit nutze ich auch bei meiner Tätigkeit als Unternehmer."

**"LEAVING MY COMFORT ZONE AND ENTERING ANOTHER ELEMENT...**

"SORTIR DE MA ZONE DE CONFORT ET ENTRER DANS UN AUTRE ÉLÉMENT...

"ICH GEHE AUS MEINER KOMFORTZONE HERAUS UND BETRETE ANDERE SPHÄREN...

... that's how I become more aware, more creative, more efficient."

... c'est ce qui me permet de développer davantage de conscience, de créativité et de performance."

... so kann ich noch aufmerksamer, kreativer und besser werden."

**A flight monitoring system capable of alerting the pilot through vibrations on his arms.**

Système de surveillance du domaine de vol capable d'alerter le pilote par des vibrations sur les bras.

Flugüberwachungssystem, das den Piloten durch Vibrationen am Arm warnt.

**Nylon fiber clothing described as "intelligent" as it keeps the pilot's body temperature stable.**

Vêtements en fibres nylon qualifiées d'"intelligentes" car elles stabilisent la température corporelle du pilote.

Kleidung aus "intelligenten" Nylonfasern für eine stabile Körpertemperatur des Piloten.

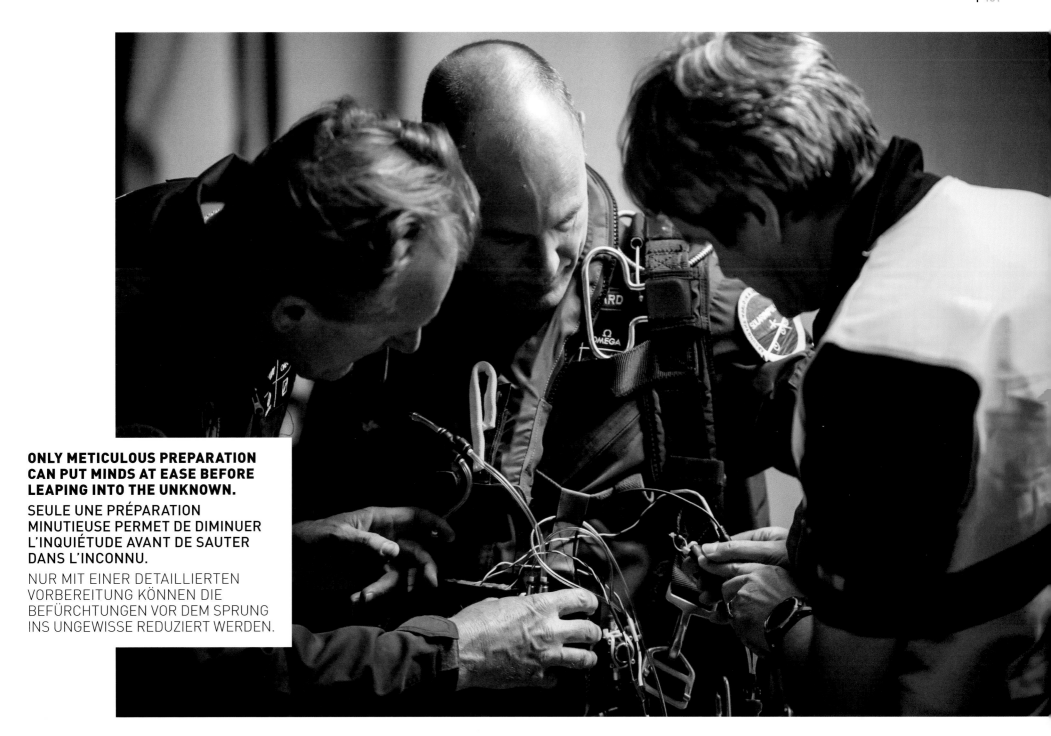

**ONLY METICULOUS PREPARATION CAN PUT MINDS AT EASE BEFORE LEAPING INTO THE UNKNOWN.**

SEULE UNE PRÉPARATION MINUTIEUSE PERMET DE DIMINUER L'INQUIÉTUDE AVANT DE SAUTER DANS L'INCONNU.

NUR MIT EINER DETAILLIERTEN VORBEREITUNG KÖNNEN DIE BEFÜRCHTUNGEN VOR DEM SPRUNG INS UNGEWISSE REDUZIERT WERDEN.

**HOW WILL THE SYSTEMS ON SUCH
A NOVEL AIRPLANE PERFORM?**

COMMENT SE COMPORTERONT
LES SYSTÈMES DE CET AVION
AUSSI NOVATEUR?

WIE WERDEN SICH DIE SYSTEME
IN DIESEM INNOVATIVEN FLUGZEUG
VERHALTEN?

**How do you manage long distance flights
and anticipate all scenarios?**

Comment gérer des vols de longues distances
et prévoir tous les scénarios?

Wie wickelt man Langstreckenflüge ab und
nimmt alle Szenarien vorweg?

**How do you cross oceans when you can't predict
flight conditions near the destination?**

Comment traverser les océans quand on ne peut
pas prédire les conditions de vol sur la fin de l'étape?

Wie überquert man Ozeane, wenn die
Flugbedingungen am Ende der Strecke nicht
vorhersehbar sind?

## OPERATIONAL CHALLENGE

AS WITH ALL MAJOR FIRSTS, THERE ARE NO PAST REFERENCES TO GUIDE US.

Strategies must be created from scratch. At the heart of this technological adventure, anticipation, simulation, action and emotion.

## CHALLENGE OPERATIONNEL

COMME DANS TOUTES LES GRANDES PREMIÈRES, IL N'EXISTE AUCUNE RÉFÉRENCE PRÉALABLE.

Les stratégies doivent être inventées à partir de zéro. Anticipation, simulation, action et émotion au cœur de l'aventure technologique.

## OPERATIVE HERAUS-FORDERUNG

WIE BEI ALLEN GROSSEN PREMIEREN GIBT ES KEINE VORHERIGEN REFERENZEN.

Die Strategien müssen von Grund auf neu erfunden werden. Vorausschau, Simulation, Aktion und Emotion im Zentrum des technologischen Abenteuers.

**NO HANGAR BIG ENOUGH TO HOUSE THE AIRPLANE? NO PROBLEM, THE TEAM TRAVELS WITH ITS OWN SOLUTION!**

PAS DE HANGAR ASSEZ GRAND POUR ACCUEILLIR L'AVION? QU'À CELA NE TIENNE, L'ÉQUIPE SE DÉPLACE AVEC SA PROPRE SOLUTION!

DER HANGAR IST NICHT GROSS GENUG, UM DAS FLUGZEUG ZU BEHERBERGEN? FÜR DIESEN FALL REIST DAS TEAM MIT SEINER EIGENEN LÖSUNG AN!

**Designed entirely by the team, this mobile hangar can be inflated in less than 5 hours and can protect the plane from storms and 60 mph winds.**

Entièrement conçu par l'équipe, ce hangar mobile, gonflable en moins de 5 heures, permet de protéger l'avion des intempéries et des vents de 100 km/h.

Dieser mobile Hangar wurde vollständig von dem Team entwickelt. Er kann in weniger als 5 Stunden aufgeblasen werden und schützt das Flugzeug vor schlechtem Wetter und Windgeschwindigkeiten bis zu 100 km/h.

**The plane can even recharge its batteries through the fabric of the hangar!**

Même à l'abri, l'avion peut recharger ses batteries à travers la toile du hangar!

Selbst im Schatten kann das Flugzeug seine Batterien durch das Zeltdach des Hangars aufladen!

**A STOPOVER AT AN AIRPORT OR AT
THE "MODERN MUSEUM OF ART"?**

ESCALE SUR UN AÉROPORT OU
AU "MODERN MUSEUM OF ART"?

ZWISCHENLANDUNG AM FLUGHAFEN
ODER IM "MODERN MUSEUM OF ART"?

**MOVING SOLAR IMPULSE AND ALL TECHNICAL EQUIPMENT TO THE DEPARTURE POINT OF THE MISSION.**

ACHEMINEMENT DE SOLAR IMPULSE ET DE TOUT LE MATÉRIEL TECHNIQUE SUR LE LIEU DE DÉPART DE LA MISSION.

VERLADUNG UND TRANSPORT VON SOLAR IMPULSE UND DEM GESAMTEN TECHNISCHEN MATERIAL ZUM ABFLUGORT DER MISSION.

**THE SOLAR AIRPLANE IS SPECIALLY DESIGNED TO BE DISMANTLED AND CARRIED IN THE BELLY OF A JUMBO JET.**

L'AVION SOLAIRE A ÉTÉ SPÉCIALEMENT CONÇU POUR POUVOIR ÊTRE DÉMONTÉ ET TRANSPORTÉ DANS LE VENTRE D'UN JUMBO JET.

DAS SOLARFLUGZEUG WURDE SO ENTWICKELT, DASS ES IN EINZELTEILEN IM INNERN EINES JUMBO JETS TRANSPORTIERT WERDEN KANN.

**BEFORE EVERY TAKE-OFF, THE GROUND CREW GIVES THE PLANE A COMPLETE CHECK-OVER.**

**AVANT CHAQUE DÉCOLLAGE, L'AVION EST SOUMIS À UN CHECK-UP COMPLET PAR L'ÉQUIPE AU SOL.**

VOR JEDEM ABFLUG WIRD DAS FLUGZEUG DURCH DAS BODENPERSONAL EINEM KOMPLETT-CHECK UNTERZOGEN.

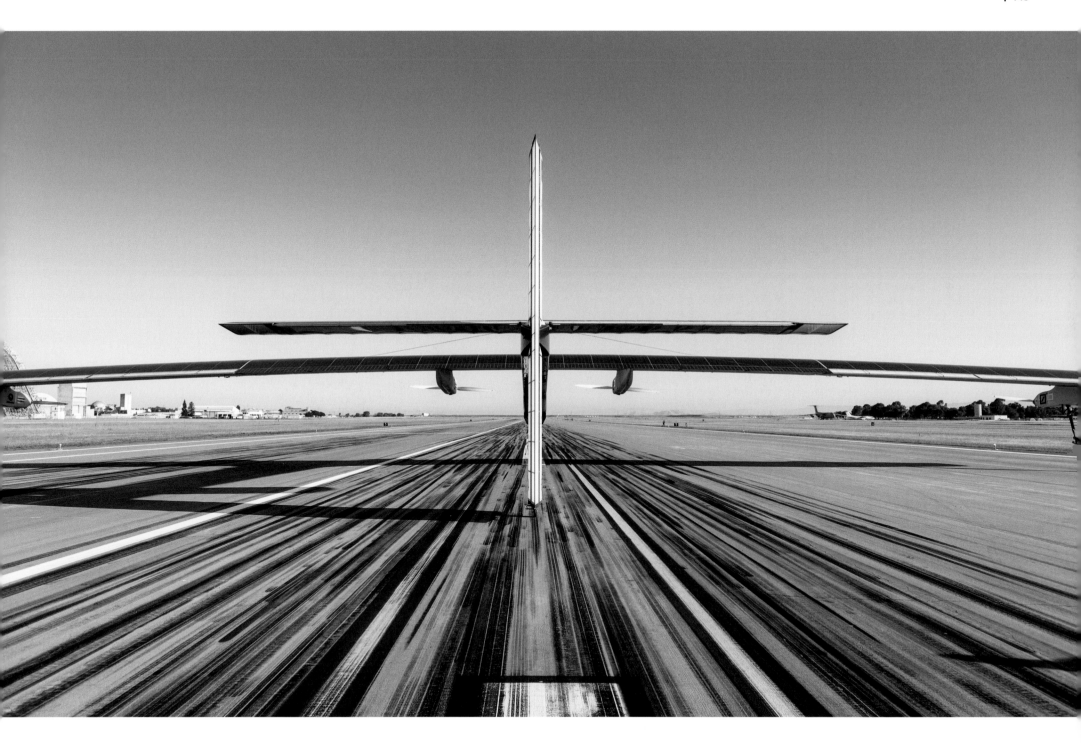

**IN CONTACT BY SATELLITE WITH MISSION CONTROL CENTER, TO MONITOR ITS ROUTE AND MANAGE ITS POWER.**

EN CONTACT PAR SATELLITE AVEC LE MISSION CONTROL CENTER, POUR LE SUIVI DE SA ROUTE ET LA GESTION DE SON ÉNERGIE.

DER PILOT STEHT PER SATELLIT IN STÄNDIGEM KONTAKT MIT DEM MISSION CONTROL CENTER UND ERHÄLT DIE ENTSPRECHENDEN INFORMATIONEN ZU FLUGROUTE UND ENERGIEVERWALTUNG.

Weathermen, mathematicians, air traffic controllers, planning engineers, flight director, a host of guardian angels to predict all possible scenarios and prepare a strategy.

Météorologues, mathématiciens, contrôleurs aériens et ingénieurs de planification, directeur de vol, autant d'anges-gardiens pour anticiper tous les scénarios possibles et élaborer une stratégie.

Meteorologen, Mathematiker, Fluglotsen, Planungstechniker und der Flugleiter gehören zu den zahlreichen „Schutzengeln", die jedes mögliche Szenario vorwegnehmen und die entsprechenden Strategien entwickeln.

**Getting a message across, capturing people's
attention, engaging the public in the adventure.**

**Communiquer un message, frapper les esprits,
emmener le public dans l'aventure.**

Die Botschaft verbreiten, einen bleibenden
Eindruck hinterlassen, die Öffentlichkeit auf
das Abenteuer mitnehmen.

**AN EPIC FLIGHT AROUND THE WORLD IN 12 STAGES IN THE NORTHERN HEMISPHERE.**

UNE ÉPOPÉE AUTOUR DU MONDE EN 12 ÉTAPES DANS L'HÉMISPHÈRE NORD.

EINE MEISTERLEISTUNG IN 12 ETAPPEN RUND UM DIE WELT AUF DER NÖRDLICHEN HALBKUGEL.

**Departing from Abu Dhabi for a journey of
over 22,000 miles, 25 days of actual flights
between March and July.**

**Départ d'Abu Dhabi pour un parcours de
36 000 kilomètres, 25 jours de vols effectifs
entre mars et juillet.**

Abflug in Abu Dhabi auf eine 36 000 Kilometer
lange Reise während 25 Flugtagen zwischen
März und Juli.

# THE ROUTE | LA ROUTE | DIE ROUTE

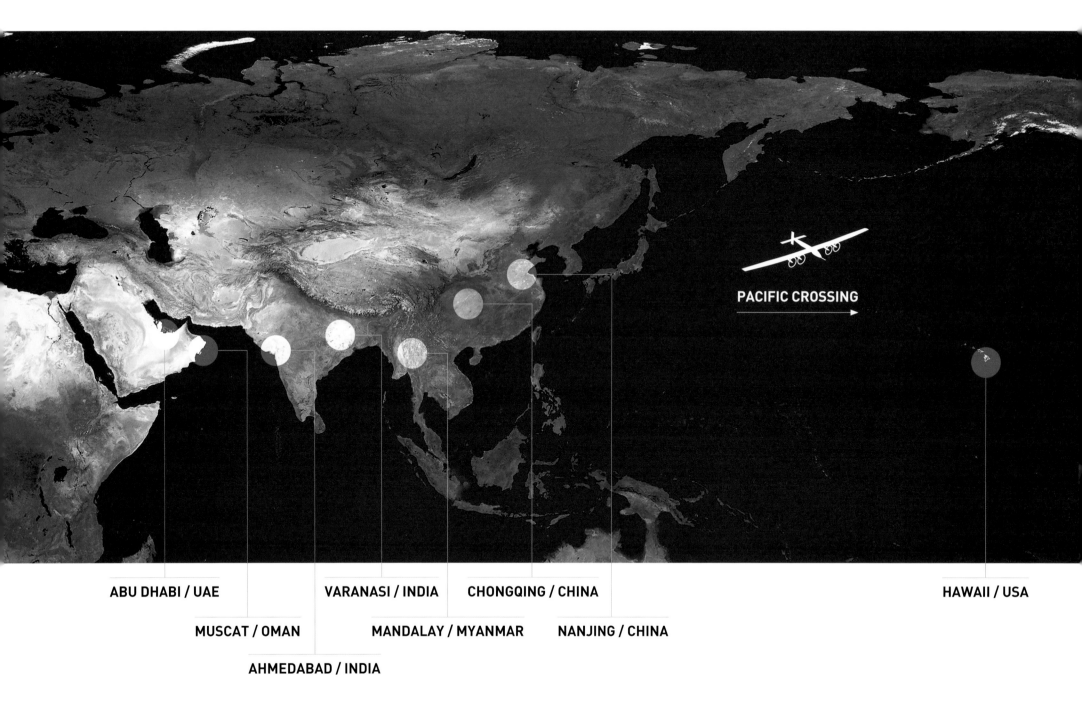

PACIFIC CROSSING

ABU DHABI / UAE        VARANASI / INDIA        CHONGQING / CHINA        HAWAII / USA

MUSCAT / OMAN        MANDALAY / MYANMAR        NANJING / CHINA

AHMEDABAD / INDIA

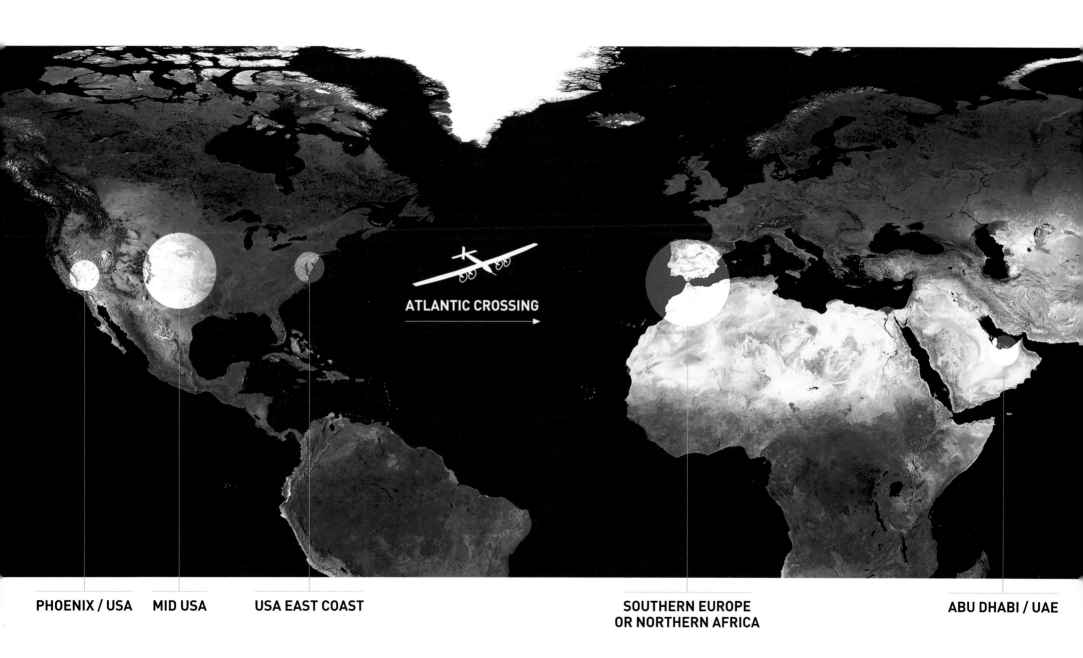

ATLANTIC CROSSING

PHOENIX / USA    MID USA    USA EAST COAST

SOUTHERN EUROPE
OR NORTHERN AFRICA

ABU DHABI / UAE

Route plan as of November 2014, subject to change and pending flight authorizations.

# A SYMBOL
# UN SYMBOLE
EIN SYMBOL

"Solar Impulse was not built to carry passengers, but to carry messages. We want to demonstrate the importance of pioneering spirit, to encourage people to question what they've always taken for granted. The world needs to find new ways of improving the quality of human life. Clean technologies and renewable forms of energy are part of the solution."

"Solar Impulse n'a pas été construit pour transporter des passagers, mais pour transporter des messages. Nous voulons démontrer l'importance de l'esprit de pionnier, encourager les gens à remettre leurs certitudes en question. Notre monde a besoin de nouvelles solutions pour améliorer la qualité de vie de l'humanité. Les technologies propres et les énergies renouvelables en font partie."

"Solar Impulse wurde nicht gebaut, um Passagiere zu befördern, sondern um Botschaften zu transportieren. Wir wollen die Bedeutung des Pioniergeistes zeigen und die Menschen auffordern, ihre sicheren Überzeugungen in Frage zu stellen. Unsere Welt braucht neue Lösungen, um die Lebensqualität der Menschheit zu verbessern. Saubere Technologien und erneuerbare Energien sind in dieser Hinsicht ein integraler Bestandteil."

**BERTRAND PICCARD**

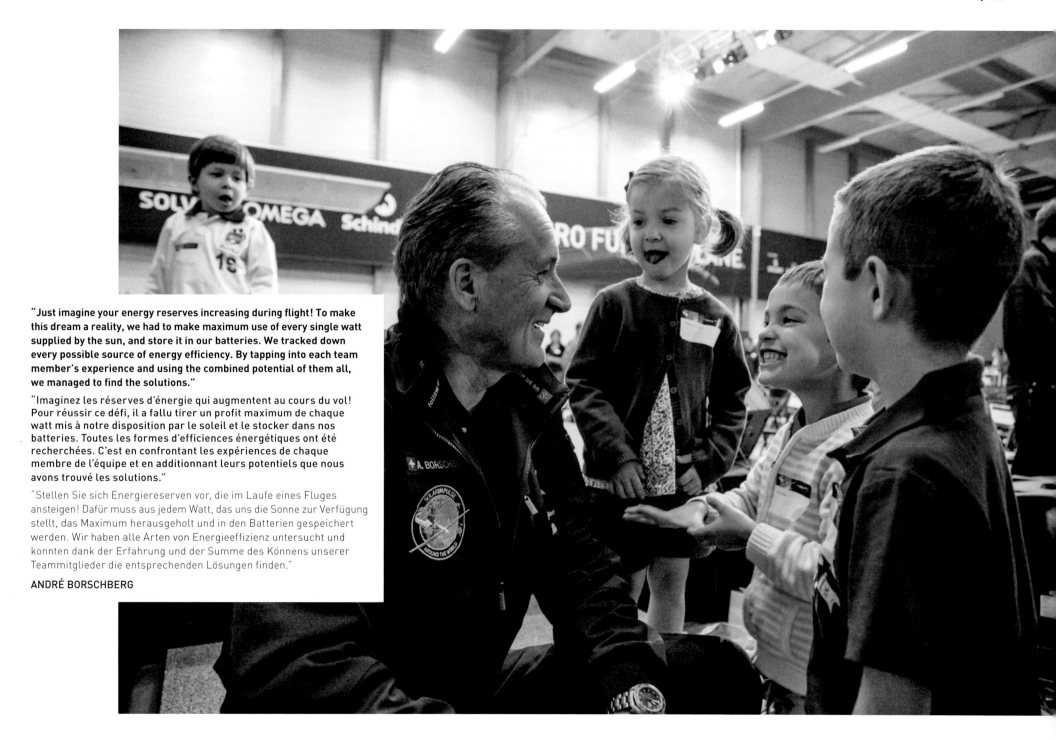

"Just imagine your energy reserves increasing during flight! To make this dream a reality, we had to make maximum use of every single watt supplied by the sun, and store it in our batteries. We tracked down every possible source of energy efficiency. By tapping into each team member's experience and using the combined potential of them all, we managed to find the solutions."

"Imaginez les réserves d'énergie qui augmentent au cours du vol! Pour réussir ce défi, il a fallu tirer un profit maximum de chaque watt mis à notre disposition par le soleil et le stocker dans nos batteries. Toutes les formes d'efficiences énergétiques ont été recherchées. C'est en confrontant les expériences de chaque membre de l'équipe et en additionnant leurs potentiels que nous avons trouvé les solutions."

"Stellen Sie sich Energiereserven vor, die im Laufe eines Fluges ansteigen! Dafür muss aus jedem Watt, das uns die Sonne zur Verfügung stellt, das Maximum herausgeholt und in den Batterien gespeichert werden. Wir haben alle Arten von Energieeffizienz untersucht und konnten dank der Erfahrung und der Summe des Könnens unserer Teammitglieder die entsprechenden Lösungen finden."

ANDRÉ BORSCHBERG

THE ADVENTURE THAT SHOWS
**CHANGE** IS **POSSIBLE.**

L'AVENTURE QUI PROUVE QU'**UN
CHANGEMENT** EST **POSSIBLE.**

DIESES ABENTEUER BEWEIST,
DASS **VERÄNDERUNG MÖGLICH** IST.

AFTER THE INDUSTRIAL AND
DIGITAL REVOLUTION, THE **CLEAN
TECH REVOLUTION** BRINGS **HOPE**
AND INNOVATIVE SOLUTIONS TO THE
**CHALLENGES FACING MANKIND.**

APRÈS LES RÉVOLUTIONS INDUSTRIELLE
ET INFORMATIQUE, LA **RÉVOLUTION
CLEAN TECH** APPORTE UN **ESPOIR**
ET DES SOLUTIONS INNOVANTES AUX
**DÉFIS DE L'HUMANITÉ.**

NACH DER INDUSTRIELLEN UND
DIGITALEN REVOLUTION BEDEUTET DIE
**CLEAN TECH REVOLUTION HOFFNUNG**
UND INNOVATIVE LÖSUNGSANSÄTZE
FÜR DIE **HERAUSFORDERUNGEN
DER MENSCHHEIT.**

ONLY **MASSIVE POPULAR ENTHUSIASM**
FOR **CLEAN ENERGY** WILL GIVE
GOVERNMENTS THE COURAGE TO
**TAKE THE NECESSARY DECISIONS.**

SEUL UN **ENTHOUSIASME POPULAIRE**
DE GRANDE ENVERGURE EN FAVEUR
DES **ÉNERGIES PROPRES** DONNERA
AUX GOUVERNEMENTS LE COURAGE DE
**PRENDRE LES DÉCISIONS NÉCESSAIRES.**

NUR EINE BREIT GEFÄCHERTE
**BEGEISTERUNG INNERHALB DER
BEVÖLKERUNG** FÜR DIE NUTZUNG
**SAUBERER ENERGIEN** WIRD DIE
REGIERUNGEN ERMUTIGEN, **NOTWENDIGE
ENTSCHEIDUNGEN ZU TREFFEN.**

**THE FUTURE CAN BE WRITTEN** IN RENEWABLE ENERGY. AN ADVENTURE WE CAN ALL TAKE PART IN **TOGETHER.**

**LE FUTUR PEUT S'ÉCRIRE** À L'ÉNERGIE RENOUVELABLE. UNE AVENTURE À POURSUIVRE TOUS **ENSEMBLE.**

**DIE ZUKUNFT KANN** MIT ERNEUERBAREN ENERGIEN **GESCHRIEBEN WERDEN.** DIESES ABENTEUER SOLLTEN WIR ALLE **GEMEINSAM** BESTREITEN.

# TEAM | ÉQUIPE | TEAM

**ENERGY & PROPULSION**

MARTIN PFISTER
AMIR MARREI
SÉBASTIEN DEMONT
STEFAN BRÖNNIMAN
ANTOINE TOTH
GAËL LEMOINE
HANS WUESTEMANN
KARL OSEN
JOËL SUNNIER
DAVID GLASSEY
PETER SAX
THOMAS SEILER
JOSEF NIEDERNHUBER
SIYARAM BHATT
UELI KRAMER
DENIS GLASSEY
PATRICK EBERLE
DANIEL FROSSARD
DYLAN GORTON

**PRODUCTION**

EUGEN SCHMID
MIELE OLIVER
STEVE WASEM
THOMAS STREULI
JEAN-MARIE FRAGNIÈRE
JÜRG BIRKENSTOCK
ALESSANDRO CASAGRANDE
ISABELLE KECK
ROLF MEIER
CYRILL HUNZIKER
JEAN-MICHEL COURCOUX
MARTIN MEYER
CHRISTOPHE DANSART
MICHAEL STÄHLI
CLAUDE-ALAIN JACOT
MARC LIENHARD
MICHAEL SCHERDEL
RAMON SCHWEIZER
JONATHAN GIRARDIN
NICOLAS ACHA-ORBEA
PETER STEGOVEC
BAPTISTE LE MOING
STEFAN STADELMANN
CYRIL BRUNNER
WILFRIED BADER
JAKOB RECK
STÉPHANE CLERC
JONATHAN MERLET
SIMON WYSS
JULIEN MEUNIER
ROBERT LEU
PETER SCHINDLER
DAVID FANKHAUSER
DANIEL KOBER
BERTRAND CARDIS
STEFAN SCHÜCHTER

**GRAPHIC DESIGN & PHOTOGRAPHS**

JEAN REVILLARD
OLGA STEFATOU
ANNA PIZZOLANTE
CHRISTOPHE CHAMMARTIN
FREDERIC MERZ
NIELS ACKERMANN
FRED PESSE
JERÔME BONTRON
LOREDANA SERRA
YASHKA STEINER

ANDRÉ BORSCHBERG          BERTRAND PICCARD

**GROUND CREW**

LORAN REYMOND
DANIEL RAMSEIER
GIL STAUFFER
DAVID CAHEN
AXEL LANCÉ
ROLF WEISS
DAMIEN PIGNATARO
KEVIN RENGGLI
JIM WUEST
THIERRY GROS
ANDRÉ JAGGI
IAN NASH
CHARLY PÉTAIN
GUILHEM GINESTE
STEFAN LUDWIG
ANTONY SIMMINS
DAVID GERMANN
PIETER QUINTENS
GORAN CHATELUS
STEFAN WIELAND
ALEXANDER OSEN
JULIEN STERVINOU
RAIS BAHER
GUY MOREX
STÉPHANE COLLET
MARION PERRET
RANDI ERIKSEN
DIDIER PISTAT
JEAN-MARC BUDRY
JULIEN BERTHOUD
PHILIPPE MANUEL
CATHERINE ZANGA
LAURENT WUELSER
SAMUEL DEPRAZ
OLIVIER LOUBERSAC
CLAUDE VANZELLA
RICHARD LAVANCHY
ODILE RABLAT
PHILIPPE ROFFLER
RAPHAËLLE NICOLET

**FLIGHT TESTS & MISSIONS**

MARKUS SCHERDEL
RAYMOND CLERC
MICHAEL ANGER
ANDREAS FÜRLINGER
CHRISTOPH SCHLETTIG
JEAN-LUC SCHORER
LÉONE-AURE BES
PHILIPP HEINEMANN
CLAUDE NICOLLIER
HEINER NEUMANN
DAMIEN RIZET
NILS RYSER
MANUEL HAAG
NIKLAUS GERBER
STÉPHANE YONG
TAHAN PANGARIBUAN
ROGERS SMITH
CHRISTOPHE ETTER
BRIAN JONES
LAILA FATHI
ROGER JEGERLEHNER
WIM DE TROYER
MARTIN BRYNER
YVES-ANDRÉ FASEL
LUC TRULLEMANS
CHRISTOPHE BÉESAU
ADELINE HOCHEDEZ
MICHEL MASSEREY
URSULA FRANKHOF

**MULTIMEDIA**

BENJAMIN MAILLEFER
BOSSON ANTOINE
DIDIER HUMBERT
JACKY SANDERS
EMMANUEL GRIPON
THOMAS SZCZEPANSKI
LAURENT KAESER
GERVALLA DAFINA
SIGNE GREJSEN NISSEN
RADU MARMAZIU
DAVID GRAND-GUILLAUME
DAVID PATTHEY
MIRKO TOPPANO
HELENA HUMPHREY
DAMIEN NAIMI
CYRILLE PIERRE
NATHALIE KAESER
JÓN BJÖRGVINSSON
FABIEN WOHLSCHLAG
NICOLAS ZANGHI
CONOR LENNON

**CONFIGURATION & STRUCTURE**

DIDAC ZURITA
PETER FREI
MARGRET NEUENSCHWANDER
GERMÁN PORRAS
HANNES ROSS
MARTIN HEPPERLE
RICHARD LEBLOIS
ANDREA CHIELLINI
GERI PILLER
MICHAEL MCGRATH
BERND KAUTT
ELIAS DOMEISEN
CHRISTIAN STUDER
LUKAS STAUB
JEAN-MARIE BLAIRON
ARNE VOLLAN
MARCO NIEDERBERGER
ADRIAN BRÜLLMAN
ANDREA CAMBRUZZI
TOMAS FARIÑAS
SANDRA OBERHOLLENZER
OLIVER ENSSLIN
PEER FRANK
DOMINIK DUSEK
CHRISTIAN QUAGLIOTTI
JÖRG SPICHTIG
SERGIO BELTRAN
GERARDO FASANO
RALPH PAUL
EWALD REGENSCHEIT
FABIEN MANDRILLON
YVES HELLER
SEBASTIAN THIEL
DAVID OLDANI
PHILIPPE LAUPER
PAUL METZLER
ENRIQUE GUINALDO
JACQUES PEUGEOT
JAVIER SOTO
FELIX VON GYNZ-REKOWSKI
JONAS SCHÄR
PRZEMYSLAW LEKSTON
KEVIN SCHELLINGER
PASCAL BARMET
STEFAN PFAMMATTER
MATTEO BARTOLLINI
BORIS KÖLMEL
EDUARDO SÁNCHEZ
FREDERICK TISCHHAUSER
HERBERT LIESER
ROBERT FRAEFEL
JENS MENZEL
MARCUS BASIEN
BJOERN MÜLLER
BRUNO NEININGER
JOSE IGNACIO MAESTRA
SIMON BODMER

**MARKETING & COMMUNICATION**

GREGORY BLATT
MICHÈLE PICCARD
CAROLE MARGUERON
CONSTANTIN DE NASSAU
BRUNO BOEHM
VINCENT COLEGRAVE
MARC DE BORST
MARIE BARBIER-MUELLER
ALEXANDRA GINDROZ
MASSOUMA ZIAI
ELÂ BORSCHBERG
CLAUDIA DURGNAT
ALEXANDRA GRAND D'HAUTEVILLE
VIKTORIA DIJAKOVIC
ALAIN ANDREY
ALENKA ZIBETTO
ANNE-LAURE PERRIER
MARTA LOPES
PHILIP NORRIS

**FINANCES & ADMINISTRATION**

PHILIPPE RATHLE
MARCEL AEBERLI
ANNE-CHRISTINE PERREN BENZINE
BRIGITTE ZAHND
ELIANE RASCH
DIRK MÜHLEMANN
BARBARA BRUNI
ALAIN PIRLOT
TAMARA PELÈGE
LORRAINE DUPART DOMENJOZ

# PARTNERS | PARTENAIRES | PARTNER

## MAIN PARTNERS

**SOLVAY**
Advanced Materials
Solution Provider

**OMEGA**
Technology Provider
and Time Keeper

**SCHINDLER**
Technology For Clean Mobility

**ABB**
Power and Automation Partner

## OFFICIAL PARTNERS

**SWISS RE CORPORATE
SOLUTIONS**
Official Insurance Provider

**BAYER MATERIALSCIENCE**
Official Partner

**ALTRAN**
Engineering Partner

## OFFICIAL INTERNET
TECHNOLOGY PARTNER

**GOOGLE**
Official Internet Technology Partner

## OFFICIAL NATIONAL PARTNER

**SWISSCOM**
National Telecom Partner

## OFFICIAL SUPPORTERS

**AIR LIQUIDE ADVANCED
TECHNOLOGIES**
Official Pilot Support Partner

**CLARINS**
Official Supporter

**DASSAULT SYSTEMES**
Official 3D Experience Partner

**MCKINSEY & COMPANY**
Knowledge Partner

**SEMPER**
Official Supporter

**VICTORINOX**
Swiss Knife Supplier

## OFFICIAL NATIONAL
SUPPORTERS

**BKW ENERGIE AG**
Official National Supporter

**SERVICES INDUSTRIELS
DE GENEVE**
Official National Supporter

**TOYOTA AG**
Swiss Hybrid Supporter

## OFFICIAL SUPPLIERS

**DECISION SA**
Composite Materials

**ETEL**
Electric Motor Propulsion

**LANTAL TEXTILES**
Pneumatic Comfort System

**MEYER BURGER TECHNOLOGY AG**
Official Supplier

**NESTLE HEALTH SCIENCE**
Pilots' Nutrition and Dietary
Supplier

**SIEMENS PLM SOFTWARE**
Official Supplier

**SOLARMAX**
Official Supplier

**SUNPOWER**
Solar Cells Supplier

**VACUUMSCHMELZE GmbH**
Permanent Magnets

## OFFICIAL NATIONAL SUPPLIERS

**LA SEMEUSE**
Coffee Supplier

**HIRSLANDEN**
Medical Advisors

**STROMER**
E-Bike Supplier

## INSTITUTIONAL PARTNERS

**EPFL**
Official Scientific Advisor

**SWISS CONFEDERATION**
Institutional Partner

## AERONAUTICAL PARTNERS

**ACI EUROPE**
Airport Council International
Europe

**ACI WORLD**
Airport Council International World

**DASSAULT AVIATION**
Aircraft Manufacturer Advisor

**EMPA**
Swiss Federal Laboratories for
Materials Science and Technology

**ESA**
European Space Agency

**EUROCONTROL**
Air Traffic Control Partner

**IATA**
International Air Transport
Association

**ICAO**
International Civil Aviation
Organization

**SKYGUIDE**
Air Traffic Control Partner

## AROUND THE WORLD PARTNERS

**ABU DHABI**
Arrival and Departure Host City

**MASDAR**
Arrival and Departure Host Partner

**MONACO**
Mission Control Host City

**PRINCE ALBERT II OF MONACO
FOUNDATION**
Mission Control Host Partner

**ADITYA BIRLA GROUP**
India Host Partner

## SPECIALIZED PARTNERS

**ABAECHERLI DRUCK**
Printing Specialist

**AEROFEM**
Engineering Consultant and
Software Support Specialist

**AIR ENERGY**
Lithium Batteries Management

**AIR STAR**
Mobile Hangar Construction
Specialist

**ALR**
Design Expert

**AVESCO RENT**
Equipment Rental Specialist

**CELEROTON**
Frequency Converter Specialist

**COBHAM SATCOM**
Satellite Communication System
Specialist

**COBHAM SURVEILLANCE**
Telemetry Specialist

**CONNOVA**
Manufacturer of Composite Parts

**CONSTELLIUM**
Aluminium Material Specialist

**COURVOISIER**
Printing Specialist

**CREATIVES**
Mobile Application Partner

**DLR**
Ground Vibration Specialist

**DRAKA FILECA**
Electrical Cable Specialist

**DRIVETEK**
Electrical Systems

**EADS DEFENSE & SECURITY**
Helicopter Support

**EURAAUDIT SUISSE**
Auditors

**EUREKA CORPORATION**
IT Support Specialist

**EUROPAVIA (Switzerland)**
Eurocopter Distributor,
Swiss Helicopter Group

**FIDEXAUDIT REVISION SA**
Auditors

**FIDULEM**
Chartered Accountants

**FLY-IN BALLOONS**
Mobile Hangar Developer

**FRIDERICI SPECIAL**
Special Transport

**GONTHIER & SCHNEEBERGER**
Insurance Broker

**HERPA**
Model Specialist

**HS TURBOMASCHINEN**
Turbo Compressor for the
Pressurization System

**IDC**
Gear Manufacturing Specialist

**INFOMANIAK NETWORK**
Website Hosting

**INSTITUT DE MICROTECHNIQUE
DE L'UNIVERSITE DE NEUCHATEL**
Photovoltaic Cells Expert

**INSTITUT ROYAL
METEOROLOGIQUE DE BELGIQUE**
Meteorology and Routing

**INTER-TRANSLATIONS**
Translations Specialist

**JEPPESEN**
Aeronautical Integrated Solutions

**LANITZ-PRENA FOLIEN FACTORY**
Film and fabric cover specialist

**LE TRUC**
Motion Design

**LISTA OFFICE**
Mission Room Provider

**LUCERNE UNIVERSITY OF
APPLIED SCIENCE AND ARTS**
Study of Fluid/Structure Interaction

**MAKROART**
Large Scale Digital Printing

**METEOSUISSE**
Meteorology specialist

**MICHELIN**
Tire Development

**MICRO-BEAM**
Electric Motor Driver

**MOEBEL PFISTER**
VIP Lounge Provider

**NIKON AG**
Photographic and Video Material
Specialist

**NUESSLI SCHWEIZ AG**
Temporary Construction Specialist

**ON AIR**
Swift Broadband
Satellite Connectivity

**PIELLEITALIA**
Team & Project Clothing

**PLASMA COMMUNICATION**
Technical Video Services

**P&TS MARQUES**
Intellectual Property Protection

**QNX SOFTWARE SYSTEMS**
Real-time Operating
System Provider

**RUAG AEROSPACE**
Aerodynamics and
Structure Testing

**SAVEURS & COULEURS**
Catering Specialist

**SKF (SWITZERLAND)**
Bearing Technology, Analytic
Modeling, Virtual Testing

**SOURIAU**
Connectors Specialist

**SQS**
Swiss Association for Quality
and Management Systems

**TAVERNIER TSCHANZ**
Legal Advisor

**THE MATHWORKS**
Matlab Software Specialist

**TOYOTA MATERIAL HANDLING
(Switzerland)**
Handling Material Specialist

**TRANSCAT PLM**
Software Support

**TRIADEM SOLUTIONS**
Hardware and Software Specialist

**UDITIS**
Guest Lead Event Solution

**VECTRONIX**
Night Vision Goggles specialist

**ZHAW, ZURICH UNIVERSITY
OF APPLIED SCIENCES**
Meteorology consultant

**SUPPLIERS AND OTHERS**

**AC PROPULSION**

**AD & C**

**ALTIUM**

**BERINGER**

**BONTRON & CO**

**LAKE GENEVA REGION**

**LA SOURIS VERTE**

**LUMIERE NOIRE**

**METTLER-TOLEDO**

**MODECO**

**MOUNTAIN HIGH E&S CO**

**ON TOP**

**REZO.CH**

**RTS – RADIO TELEVISION SUISSE**

**TRANSMETRA**

# FOUNDATION | FONDATION | STIFTUNG

**FOUNDATION BOARD**
CONSEIL DE FONDATION
STIFTUNGSRAT

Stefan Catsicas

Patrick de Preux

Bertrand Piccard

André Borschberg

**ANGELS AND DONORS**
ANGES ET DONATEURS
ANGELS UND SPENDER

Daniel Aegerter

Henri & Daïné d'Arenberg

Ariane Spiedel-Bodmer

Henriette Bezzola-Bodmer

Hans C. Bodmer

Bertrand Bory

Christine & Dominique Brustlein

Patrick Delarive

Rolland-Yves Mauvernay
Thierry Mauvernay

Denis Defforey

Michel Firmenich

Philip Firmenich

Eric Freymond

André & Rosalie Hoffmann

Urs Hubacher

Fredy & Regula Lienhard

Thérèse Meier

Nicolas Oltramare

Nicolas Wavre

Fondation Pro Techno

Fondation Juchum

Prix Clarins Men

**PATRONS**
PARRAINS
PATEN

Dr. Joseph Ackermann

Buzz Aldrin

Yann Arthus-Bertrand

Sir Richard Branson

James Cameron

Paulo Coelho

Peter Diamandis

HSH Albert II de Monaco

Jean-Louis Etienne

Al Gore

Nicolas Hulot

Erik Lindbergh

Hubert Reeves

Robert Swan

Jean Verne

Don Walsh

Elie Wiesel

Richard Wiese

**SUPPORTERS' PROGRAM**
PROGRAMME DES SUPPORTERS
SUPPORTER PROGRAMM

Pioneers

François-Xavier Bagnoud

Noan Borel

Milia Borel

Philippe Bouriez

Faiza & Alexander Brunner

République et Canton du Jura

Ingrid & Jean-Claude Chassot

Commune de Chêne-Bourg

Commune de Collonge-Bellerive

Dr. Susanne Gruenenberg

Famille JMGreindl

Elmar Jochheim

Ville de Lausanne

Regula Lienhard

Fredy et Regula Lienhard

Markus Müller

Anne et Rafik Rathle

Louisa Svenja Moritz Ryf

Nany Nany'bis Generation

Râ

**EXPLORERS,**
**ADVENTURERS, FRIENDS**

Find the full list on
**www.solarimpulse.com**

# PHOTOS | IMAGES | BILDER

# IMPRESSUM

**OFFICIAL PHOTOGRAPHERS**
PHOTOGRAPHES OFFICIELS
OFFIZIELLE FOTOGRAFEN

www.rezo.ch

Jean Revillard

Niels Ackermann

Fred Mertz

Anna Pizzolante

Olga Stefatou

Christophe Chammartin

**FREELANCER PHOTOGRAPHERS**
PHOTOGRAPHES INDEPENDANTS
EXTERNE FOTOGRAFEN

Francis Demange

Fabrice Coffrini

Alain Ernault

Dominique Favre

Laure Geerts

Stéphane Gros

Laurent Kaeser

Benjamin Maillefer

Hector Martin Moreno

Martin Ruetschi

Driss Benmalek Toto K.

Archives Piccard

Archives Parrains SI

Festival Jules Verne
by A.Childeric/
© www.julesverne.org/
All rights reserved

**COMPUTER GRAPHICS**
IMAGES DE SYNTHESE
COMPUTERGRAFIK

Le Truc

**TECHNICAL DRAWINGS**
DESSINS TECHNIQUES
TECHNISCHE ZEICHNUNGEN

Solar Impulse

**PROJECT DIRECTION**
DIRECTION DE PROJET
PROJEKTLEITUNG

Michèle Piccard

**ARTISTIC DIRECTION**
DIRECTION ARTISTIQUE
KÜNSTLERISCHE LEITUNG

Jérôme Bontron

**EDITORIAL DESIGN**
CONCEPTION EDITORIALE
REDAKTIONELLE GESTALTUNG

Michèle Piccard

**GRAPHIC DESIGN**
CONCEPTION GRAPHIQUE
GRAFIKDESIGN

Bontron & Co – Geneva
Loredana Serra
www.bontron.ch

**TEXT WRITTEN BY**
REDACTION TEXTES
TEXTREDAKTION

Michèle Piccard
Bertrand Piccard

**TRANSLATORS**
TRADUCTEURS
ÜBERSETZER

Helene Kubasky (Deutsch)
Straco Translation (English)
Max Bishop (English)

**PRINTER**
IMPRESSION
DRUCK

Courvoisier – Bienne – Switzerland
Jean-Marc Peltier
www.courvoisier.ch

**SOLAR IMPULSE S.A.**
PSE-C, EPFL Scientific Park
CH-1015 Lausanne, Switzerland
www.solarimpulse.com

Printed in compliance with ISO
environmental standard 14001

Imprimé dans le respect de
la norme environnementale
ISO 14001.

Umweltfreundlicher Druck
nach Norm ISO 14001.